DAILY MAIL CROSSWORD BOOK
VOLUME TWO

Also published

Daily Mail Quick Crossword Book

Daily Mail
Crossword Book
Volume Two

HEADLINE

First published in 1997
by HEADLINE BOOK PUBLISHING

7 9 10 8

ISBN 0 7472 5702 7

Typeset by Michael Mepham, Frome, Somerset
Printed and bound in Great Britain by
Clays Ltd, St Ives plc

HEADLINE BOOK PUBLISHING
A division of Hodder Headline PLC
338 Euston Road
London NW1 3BH

1

ACROSS

1 Where to find somewhere to live around London (4,8)
8 Writing skill needed to dispose of lice (7)
9 Badly cut nail making one mad (7)
11 Front-of-house promotions (10)
12 A head turning to see fish (4)
14 Laid down on entering the church (8)
16 Modern centre arranged back to front (6)
17 Money can be a problem (3)
19 It gets one going at a lower level (6)
21 Red Doris gets involved in a riot (8)
24 She is behind an invitation to view (4)
25 Getting soft and stupid in university finally achieves nothing (10)
27 Dodge back to see first goalkeeper's success (7)
28 A Northern Ireland strike backed by the beasts (7)
29 Excellent under strain in reporting action completed (7,5)

DOWN

1 The rash fellow angered the boss (7)
2 Michael can do a turn without thinking (10)
3 Splits with church leader about sins (8)
4 Where one's high yet might be down (6)
5 Man bound for New York (4)
6 Squeeze out the next non-starter being offensive (7)
7 The French girl who forced one to go into the river (12)
10 Hire a building for a school (12)
13 Political activity giving one quite a turn (10)
15 No use taking religious instruction from an old priest (3)
18 Limit moves by worker prepared to fight (8)
20 Body of soldiers ordered to protect an oil platform (7)
22 After the depression disposed of food with teeth (7)
23 Spread out (6)
26 Turn it up very loud to make a row (4)

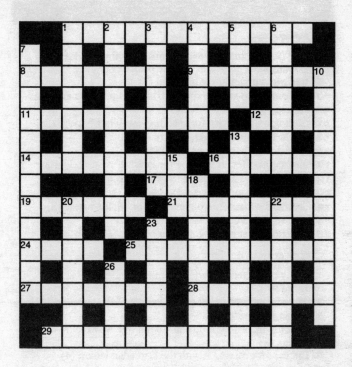

2

ACROSS

6 Rule riot out and move it deviously having a hidden agenda (8,6)
9 Sent out with a big smile (6)
10 Somewhere to stay mixing old drink with ginger and soda starters (8)
11 Finding bottom price for each move is a nuisance (8)
13 Ask to be a member of the party (6)
15 Work here when no longer skating (6)
17 One might offer an opening for Pearl (6)
19 Stone or wood attracting a large reduction (6)
20 Setback for a girl after always backing the right (8)
22 Grub tins perhaps not big enough for what's inside (8)
24 Pace in which one takes things on the move (6)
26 Buyer or seller of a royal house? (8,6)

DOWN

1 Hardy character achieving no fame as no-good legal figure (4,3,7)
2 Came across one being put up as part of the collection (4)
3 Get angry at restraint (6)
4 Cunning inclusion of dirt on soldier in a way that reveals smears (8)
5 The case for mixing it with the European Union (4)
7 Former pupil not in time to become devoted to religious life (6)
8 Get in varied tea cooked with no meat in it (10,4)
12 No good – it doesn't even begin to be permissible (5)
14 One of those exercising political power (5)
16 Time for fun that can rival riot (8)
18 Fear of becoming the last soldier in battle (6)
21 Room in church for an undercover line (6)
23 Dismiss for drink (4)
25 Somewhere to exercise when not yet 15 (4)

ACROSS

1 Ruined Edward shortly returning with the widow (8)
5 Protection from the glare that shows a way to hell (6)
9 Top European performer a heavenly guide (4,4)
10 Not having finished growing fruit (6)
12 River that's quick to cross – don't laugh! (4)
13 The nicest Reds can give it to you straight (10)
15 No restrictions on travel (2,2,3,6)
19 Protect teacher in charge of craft entries (7-6)
23 Able to grasp problem in her sleep (10)
25 Like to turn it into wine (4)
28 They've been banished from French islands (6)
29 Descent from a broken pier edge (8)
30 They make a change from wearing slacks (6)
31 Performer of entertaining take-offs (8)

DOWN

1 Cancel sitting and remove from the throne (6)
2 Get together with the right friend (5)
3 Rich drunkard (4)
4 Cautious about it being seen as a hand-out (7)
6 It represents the core of the Arthurian legend (5)
7 Collapse of spider wriggling on the breeze (9)
8 Threatening to give offence with strange rites (8)
11 Admirer of attractive girls rejecting ties (4)
14 It makes a good person light-headed (4)
15 Red in trouble when the group gets round to working on a plot (9)
16 Measure of resistance round the Queen (3)
17 Being thin one's likely to get plastered (4)
18 It's sent to start cheering people in a way (8)
20 Plant in a hurry (4)
21 Complaint of one beset by mental trouble (7)
22 Nothing being held up by a flap that's long and narrow (6)
24 Not yet occupying the office one's chosen (5)
26 Not much of a fight (5)
27 She appears as if doubled up (4)

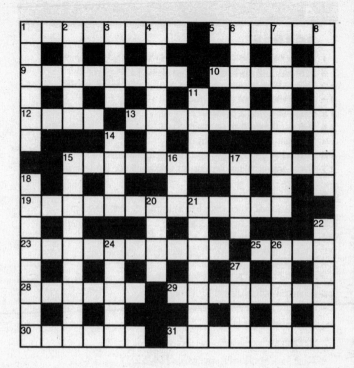

4

ACROSS

1 Remove all planes to relieve tension (5,3,3)
9 The devil in Heather making slow progress (7)
10 Take-away person returning food to get large cut (7)
11 Sparklers might leave one cold (3)
12 Adjusted with a bribe (7)
13 Very interested in getting a fix (7)
14 Drink to do up in addition (3)
15 Aimed at disrupting ways of communicating (5)
17 Swift traveller not having to pull back for something to eat (5)
18 Being simple one's in a taxi going back (5)
20 The girl that is leaving life at an unwanted level (5)
22 Say that again and it's goodbye to Wooster and Co! (3)
24 He gave humbugs for Christmas (7)
25 Picture a box with nothing in it (7)
26 Cheer the last half (3)
27 Not the corner building (7)
28 Charm Una more subtly (7)
29 Trouble about underwear revealing nothing on in the gathering light (7,4)

DOWN

1 Rise to a non-racing occasion? (4,2,2,7)
2 English farm animals said to show wit (7)
3 Some idea of following the outfit without deviating (5)
4 Take the rest of the winter to brew a thin beer (9)
5 Coming to represent a two-headed competitor (7)
6 This or that member of the family? (8,7)
7 Not much room near the beginning (6)
8 He's in business to hurry up a mission to get rid of foreign currency (6)
16 Frantic peers having to be moved during the day (9)
18 Ribs to be stewed in a restaurant (6)
19 He delivers numbers from a creditor or takes one in (7)
21 A long way to travel carrying an artist — what nonsense! (7)
23 Write an acceptable line in financial difficulty (6)
25 Take in warmth after getting cold (5)

ACROSS

1 Learner found half dead during a trick performance (7)
5 Bound to put a little weight on the piano (6)
9 Where one might be found to make a speech (7)
10 No time at work to make certain a wreath is provided first (7)
11 Hit back in standard form (3)
12 Last resort to avoid losing bedding? (5-6)
13 Yellow church hidden by rock (5)
14 Yellow rigs ruined by perfume (9)
16 Yellow quality of business fighting to take gamble (9)
17 Subdivide one and take the part that's entertaining (5)
19 It may be exercised by driver and tutor (4,7)
22 A brief measure at the rear (3)
23 Benefit from will power after departure (7)
24 Drag man round to see the old lady (7)
26 A bit of a fight to get about (6)
27 Fooled by seeing a mythical king in action (7)

DOWN

1 Be quiet when a politician rings for a cleaner (7)
2 Not feeling too well in the wind and the rain? (5,3,7)
3 River to cross between Bourne End and central Netherton (3)
4 Try to show a little commitment as teacher (5)
5 Friend with a basis for a meal that's good to eat (9)
6 Organisation for getting people married? (5)
7 Found to be committing a crime by employing communists (6,3-6)
8 They love being part of the pack (6)
12 Not qualified as thin (5)
14 Made unfriendly foreigner break a date (9)
15 Raise the purchase and have fun (5)
16 It's a hoax when nothing turns up but apple (6)
18 Bound to be leaving port this way (7)
20 Island in the Adriatic or further south (5)
21 Showed anger at the way time is taken inside (5)
25 Something of a bore? One has a point (3)

6

ACROSS

1 Triumph of the good loser (5,7)
8 Churchman keeping quiet about disagreement (7)
9 The excitement of a gamble (7)
11 Our turn to strike with dismissed rig worker (10)
12 Deliver a number while throwing fish out (4)
14 Turn out in case you can learn something from one (8)
16 Man able to jump on board (6)
17 No female could be such a cat (3)
19 Gloomy cat having something sharp stuck in (6)
21 Awful roarings where soldiers are gathered (8)
24 Trip one cancelled for those having a trying time (4)
25 Fairy ring starting to change in face of publication (10)
27 Made part of the structure put up at home (5-2)
28 Popular lawyer keeping it short (2,5)
29 In no hurry to get on with a piece of music (4,8)

DOWN

1 Search for person to make a ghostly appearance without any lead (7)
2 Having Tories around to call for some revelry (10)
3 It might be the saving of one if able to reform (8)
4 Little information on light coming in (6)
5 Said to have been instructed to get tight (4)
6 Going badly over the top in a fight situation (7)
7 Work after work (5-4,3)
10 Both sides being correct departed (5,3,4)
13 Nice bridle so tangled you wouldn't believe! (10)
15 Record endless rise of valuable material (3)
18 Spoil one spell by the sea (8)
20 Not completely prejudiced (7)
22 A church person's crass to get involved with it (7)
23 Incline in the direction of building that needs support (4-2)
26 Agitation in a fish pond (4)

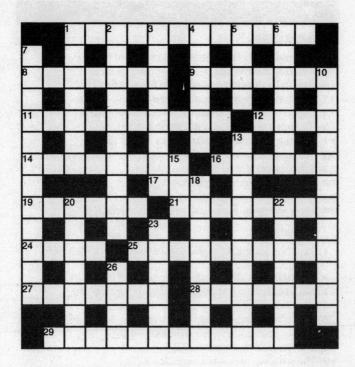

ACROSS

6 Be sensible when the motive is explained (6,2,6)
9 Run out of cover (6)
10 Gradually develop one island in ten possibly (8)
11 Harsh step towards ending enjoyment (8)
13 Deprived of free movement when in debt finally (6)
15 He kept a diary – two girls made him (6)
17 One may be drunk to show good feeling (6)
19 She gives a man a laugh (6)
20 School work put to use (8)
22 Crew's lad carelessly put down (8)
24 Use me for backing cunning manoeuvre (6)
26 Special request for an individual attraction (8,6)

DOWN

1 Smart infant told of signal at this point will quickly offer help (3,2,3,6)
2 One gets little sleep with water all round (4)
3 It's terrible cheek to accept money to interrupt (6)
4 Curb lice scurrying round the melting-pot (8)
5 Californian medical man such a gentle creature! (4)
7 Within your grasp is one right number (6)
8 It's marvellous in space! (3,2,4,5)
12 The write-up in it is not very clever (5)
14 Memento of the time before licensing hours were relaxed (5)
16 One but not two in a stable environment (8)
18 Being landed with military service in war (6)
21 Let off once when almost drained (6)
23 With the addition of some topical songs (4)
25 Look to maintain a rise (4)

8

ACROSS

1 Rate vice as being artistic (8)
5 Talk of taking an animal back round a big bend (6)
9 Easily carried away by wine and beer you've started to put brandy in (8)
10 Make a comeback after achieving a hit (6)
12 Flower girl not frequently perceived in a superior way (4)
13 Imagine what you might wear at a party (5,5)
15 Keep some breakfast to escape from a difficult situation (4,4,5)
19 Thomas's work beneath the white trees (5,4,4)
23 A lot to be gained by one refusing to return after prayer (10)
25 Stop holding up a wineglass (4)
28 Time to be dignified (6)
29 Such guidance may get a young person into films (8)
30 Bond is back with the girl when there's a choice (6)
31 Praise for having lost that bulge? (8)

DOWN

1 Drink all round with the French female on the roof (6)
2 Sign on at the end of the season in a new role (5)
3 Transport provided along urban lines (4)
4 A book able to circulate with possibly eruptive effect (7)
6 Shaped as if laid in a nest (5)
7 Given time perhaps to say a few words? (9)
8 Gasp about ales turning out to be so nice (8)
11 Bill about to give ground (4)
14 Tedious business friend going off to make a statement (4)
15 Incidental illustration of the team's lack of weight (9)
16 Nothing left when you've turned in (3)
17 Reserved volume (4)
18 Buyer's mechanical advantage (8)
20 Spot ten joining the reserve (4)
21 Being King isn't a barrier to thinking oneself omniscient (4-3)
22 Sell my bundle – it stinks (6)
24 Follow as a result of being seen wandering round the bend (5)
26 Let it be used to identify the book (5)
27 It may be consumed in the home at any time (4)

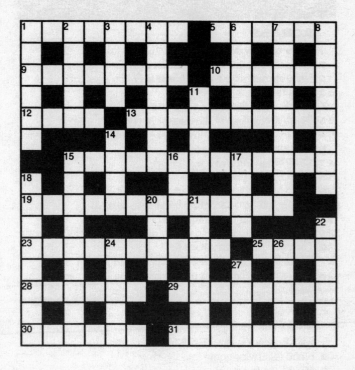

9

ACROSS

1 Order old city departure – you must be joking! (2,2,7)
9 Firm in powerful move to inflict pain (7)
10 Not objecting to a wait in hospital (7)
11 Eggs for a buck (3)
12 Go back and take the right way out (7)
13 Beastly long time in the queue (7)
14 One has to leave the snowman nevertheless (3)
15 Flavour of discrimination (5)
17 Number having a row maybe (5)
18 Get it up and you can go (5)
20 Set to hit a fellow when Father's backed off (5)
22 Go out and be back before breakfast starts (3)
24 So Laura is out for stimulation (7)
25 Crawler sent round before coming back (7)
26 The point of giving advice (3)
27 Polish backing might seem to confuse an Asian (7)
28 Sherry must give a sort of solo otherwise there's nothing in it (7)
29 Little weight attached to the girl in a Paris elopement (5,2,4)

DOWN

1 Post-Regency quarter? (6,3,6)
2 Flood otherwise going into the river (7)
3 Mocks the funny fellows – no way! (5)
4 Show regret about a measure that's unpleasant (9)
5 Each dot might represent a source of elections (7)
6 Gate man leaving dancer to change money to get something started (7,8)
7 A good man needs light when going wrong (6)
8 Give evidence during trial (6)
16 Officer of ship late for repair by the Navy (9)
18 Keep quiet baby untidy and neglected (6)
19 Frenchman giving bemused ladies the wrong handout (7)
21 Undercover rising in time of retreat (7)
23 One might be pressed to get some action (6)
25 One may be fooled by the appearance of works going up first (5)

10

ACROSS

1 Weather conditions disrupting mail, etc. (7)
5 Fears being near the end in charity (6)
9 Felt pain again when an end was attained (7)
10 Chinese dog given the German fish stew (7)
11 Reduced share (3)
12 The pile Anne made very big (11)
13 Hard work we put in one day (5)
14 Young footballer with his strange heartless lady behaving in frisky style (9)
16 In charge of an animal, in charge of a country (9)
17 Capital ring presented by a lover (5)
19 Delicious enough to steal from an orchard (11)
22 Make lace into something tasteless (3)
23 Corrupt head's involvement with cub (7)
24 Yes, worried about call for one being needed to give an injection (7)
26 Margaret providing the best spinner (3-3)
27 Hardy heroine hiding awful rig that makes her look a beast (7)

DOWN

1 South African transport bill held up in capital (7)
2 Not a good name for a top Russian (4,3,8)
3 Like hot particles of lava (3)
4 Provide with a couple of points as expected (5)
5 Chico and Lola dancing, drunk (9)
6 It could be the start of something big and shady (5)
7 Time to start a new day show (8,7)
8 Frightening with quiet movements (6)
12 Unknown having to tear madly around as a film figure (5)
14 Position of trainee having to patch side needing repair (9)
15 As a Welshman I would take a chance on failing to finish (5)
16 Hidden among the players (6)
18 Lout set off to provide possibilities of escape (7)
20 Height of a horse (5)
21 Attack in front of the film cameras (5)
25 Outfit ordered away from the troops (3)

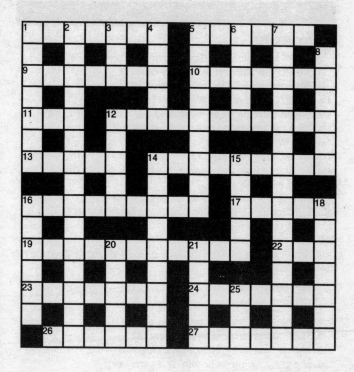

ACROSS

1 Try to be a winner without previous experience (5,7)
8 Said to give support in a dodgy deal (7)
9 Push and gasp when out of control (7)
11 Feels Nick's unusual volatility (10)
12 Where there might be animals in one's coat of arms (4)
14 Player given pad to protect crumpled suit (8)
16 Follow in the dark (6)
17 Weaken the vital fluid (3)
19 Receiving little intelligence, not of high quality (6)
21 Drop in liquidity (8)
24 Cutting a woman of loose morals (4)
25 Military unit showing no concern at being cut off (10)
27 Book to keep for future use (7)
28 One's starting to make a name (7)
29 Senior citizen back on the wagon ready to organise a happy occasion (3-6,3)

DOWN

1 Craft education continued in Italy (7)
2 Keeping things under control as a rule (10)
3 Side isn't given neat arrangement (8)
4 The endless hurry to become a singer (6)
5 She gives me up on becoming a parent (4)
6 Record rise obtained by a character giving notice (7)
7 A little drunk for a bit? (4,2,6)
10 Talking clock? That remains to be seen (4,4,4)
13 Has heading altered to be taken by the press (10)
15 Sticky result of desert rising (3)
18 Felicity raised with difficulty by father (8)
20 Anticipate there'll be something to pay when Rambling Rose is imprisoned (7)
22 Being agreeable in service? (7)
23 Walk out when you find out what's wrong (6)
26 Said not to have made a good start (4)

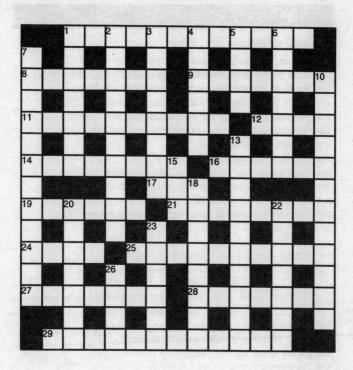

12

ACROSS

6 Nothing inside that could fool you? (6,8)

9 Veer round to the south-west instead of going straight (6)

10 Terry worries about soldiers' lists of names here (8)

11 Away before the interval to make a delivery (3-5)

13 Boy and girl losing the American cash (6)

15 Not quite right to give politicians the best cards (6)

17 Cap set in new position (6)

19 Count being one of the people (6)

20 It isn't concrete you have to take away (8)

22 Turn at a singles dance being no attraction (8)

24 Proposal to get going (6)

26 The noble matter of reform for the big drinker (5-6,3)

DOWN

1 Strong-man act that can be intimidating (4,2,8)

2 Book description endlessly vague (4)

3 Stick together in business at this point (6)

4 Heather's food intake giving protection to supporters (8)

5 God, he's the last character to use badly! (4)

7 Peer rambling round the country in a wig (6)

8 Story of moving water held by the bank (7,7)

12 Fights in scramble to bus (5)

14 Do it up and you'll feel better (5)

16 A spy cunningly conceals European one doesn't intent to stop (6-2)

18 Hound and horn (6)

21 Herb hasn't any guile (6)

23 Seen not to have gone cold (4)

25 It's turned over to me for a spell (4)

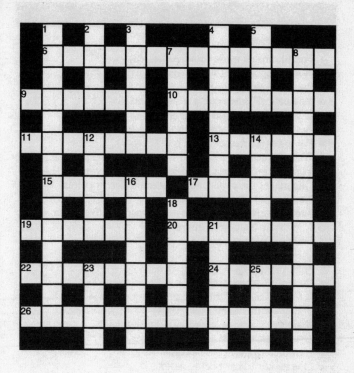

13

ACROSS

1 Friend turning aside defence work (8)
5 A bit of egotism or selfishness needed here (6)
9 Squeeze into a pad (8)
10 You can tell when one's at one's best (6)
12 It's like another instrument but not so loud (4)
13 A soldier left Mary wandering in an Irish county (10)
15 Put down a smasher as the best yet (6-7)
19 Find sanctuary in pictures with unhappily married fan (6,7)
23 Turn Paul in when a friend comes round to work (10)
25 One makes the connection between different points (4)
28 Not the real article produced by a worker of magic (6)
29 Sudden movement in distributing spoil in government (8)
30 Country in Nato manoeuvres (6)
31 Framework uncovered (8)

DOWN

1 Preserve from mischief (6)
2 It follows most of the fruit as far as it goes (5)
3 Father starting to show anger (4)
4 No hope of getting praised for reforming (7)
6 One has now made a change at either end (5)
7 Last man to shake Rome badly (9)
8 One makes light of being famous (8)
11 Remark giving point to return (4)
14 Representation of small firm in going around (4)
15 No longer needed and turned out (9)
16 Old man taking six from old king (3)
17 He's entitled to take a year off beforehand (4)
18 Knock up new names for cheese (8)
20 Friend denied support in a way that's permitted (4)
21 Pick a means of breaking new ground (7)
22 Draw conclusions about an issue (6)
24 Soft instrument (5)
26 Do it differently after one is called a fool (5)
27 The person to pay (4)

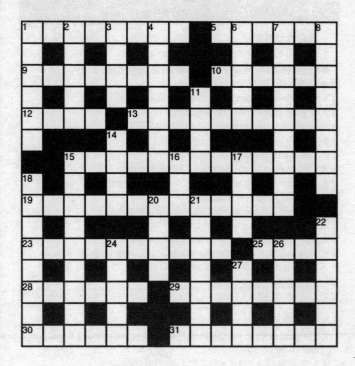

ACROSS

1 Future writer of flowery verse (7,4)
9 Case holding half a dozen of little importance (7)
10 Talks about ten rats (7)
11 One doesn't need a second service (3)
12 It puts grace into one's address (7)
13 Collide with servant and run amok (7)
14 Ring Virginia to get some eggs (3)
15 Cited amendment in the order (5)
17 Uncovered in the kitchen a kedgeree dish (5)
18 Service trainee about to get the date wrong (5)
20 Capital judge of beauty (5)
22 No way for the winner to achieve growth (3)
24 Winding rope round an admirer of the ungodly (7)
25 They're very easy to catch in photographs (7)
26 Englishman in Australia returning to clean up (3)
27 Sketch a way to gain freedom (7)
28 Paddy in a forest (7)
29 Cornered like a square (5-6)

DOWN

1 Helpful person on the beach with weapon needed for a build-up (6,3,6)
2 Get less of a blow when led around outside (7)
3 One goes on strike for the faith (5)
4 Current producer of no greater reforms (9)
5 Seat to turn over to adult (7)
6 Where North Dakota will shortly appear to be somewhere very remote (3,4,2,6)
7 Scene of the shooting (6)
8 Rise to achieve a science aim (6)
16 Carry out a piece of equipment (9)
18 Request a turnover in transport when one's made an arrest (6)
19 In a hurry for drink? Use the bell (7)
21 Bag some of the seats at Chelsea's last match (7)
23 Don't like to be given the same errand twice (6)
25 Country trip taking in Andalusia first (5)

15

ACROSS

1 Fancy cups set out (7)
5 A university god has written a book (6)
9 Compel leaderless men to join the army (7)
10 He's had a lot of experience in interpreting leasehold's terms (7)
11 Possibly one's first dip to test the water (3)
12 Not qualified to break the circle at a go (11)
13 Memorial erected to a terrier (5)
14 Ways of identifying people at first (9)
16 Common sound of time and light (9)
17 One has to give guidance to a good many (5)
19 The making of a big picture (11)
22 Holder of a poet's heart (3)
23 Taps run unusually hot here (7)
24 Belligerent army somewhere in France surrounded by water (7)
26 One's in the business of card distribution (6)
27 A case for the ministry (7)

DOWN

1 One doesn't believe cholera can start in infected surroundings (7)
2 Feel uncomfortable when nothing's said (6,2,7)
3 Don't go straight out of a feeder road (3)
4 It's a pleasure to deal with the sick (5)
5 Next to an extended team (9)
6 Union stick-up at the royal house (5)
7 What you think you can see to be deception (7,8)
8 Having gatherings for fancy dress (6)
12 Able to get ahead as a clergyman (5)
14 Not one to let the pub go (9)
15 Computer data turning up in battered tin (5)
16 Not in favour of reform as ever (6)
18 Brown being the man having to leave the circle (7)
20 Sport rally cut short in the country (5)
21 Even the thickest can display some moral principle (5)
25 Show distress with no hesitation when not affected by drink (3)

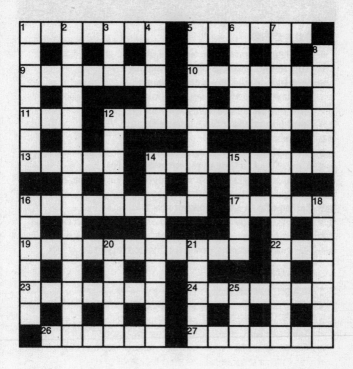

ACROSS

1 No plant person on the move as one of a group (7,5)
8 Able to be viewed as having understanding (7)
9 Stop functioning as a musical group (7)
11 Top lawyer needed to vet a printing process (4-6)
12 Save trouble by providing a vessel (4)
14 Spoil potentially great woman (8)
16 Hound and badger (6)
17 Have a Benedictine at a party to gain a woman's heart (3)
19 A great deal for one to put on as cream (6)
21 Defence material after a morning supplying shells (8)
24 Catch the bit that goes the wrong way (4)
25 Talked of odd cruises taking new routes (10)
27 Brightness at the work place when no outing will do (7)
28 Brought down to find an egg in the ditch? (4,3)
29 One puts something down for TV delivery (12)

DOWN

1 Not entirely silent thief (7)
2 MP giving support to disaffected tailors (10)
3 Held Enid to be wrong to have bird caged (8)
4 Device to have a top BBC person imprisoned (6)
5 Nonsense subject to host of new interpretations (4)
6 Falls like a terrible rain around the chief (7)
7 Misdeals suit and tries to pretend otherwise (12)
10 Severe rebuke for wearing casual clothes? (8-4)
13 Help is at hand from this person (10)
15 He finishes at the lowest level (3)
18 Powerful money put up to gain unusual ends in transport (8)
20 Do business in the street (7)
22 Cut off with water all round (7)
23 Send round another way to entertain (6)
26 Monarch the first to give village women the bird (4)

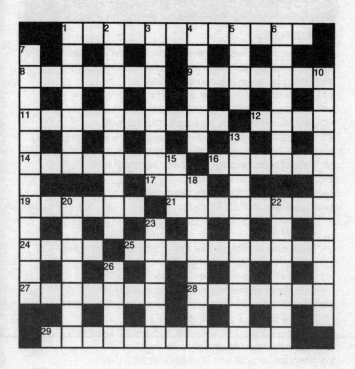

ACROSS

6 Fresh occupation until the tenant's death (3,5,2,4)
9 Meal at the pub bringing colour back all round (6)
10 Trying to disentangle more ties (8)
11 A bit different from a bikini (3-5)
13 Alarm is starting to mount in time (6)
15 Master and mistress making a complaint (6)
17 Having been given crushing treatment for some reason (6)
19 Credit one with endless approval when not an admirer (6)
20 Pulling right back to get some movement (8)
22 Get more in line (8)
24 Church person a creature devoured (6)
26 Smart city style (7,7)

DOWN

1 Man, nice trainer, turned into experienced navigator (7,7)
2 A singer with no following (4)
3 Order of last month always on the way up (6)
4 Passage of power in the Civil Service (8)
5 Record turnover – above American, what's more! (4)
7 Dog of a crossword compiler! (6)
8 Those who achieve them are well known to be rich (4,3,7)
12 Show the way one can get into the story (5)
14 Spectacular action to hold back growth (5)
16 One gives orders for nonsense at police department to be raised (8)
18 The very thing that is left out! (6)
21 Charge copper in difficult case (6)
23 River snake making a harsh noise (4)
25 Water is expelled from fruit (4)

18

ACROSS

1 No move to provide security of late (8)
5 Display in a dive (6)
9 Pipe providing a place for experimenting in money (8)
10 Rob can possibly make a copy (6)
12 She's beginning to show some light (4)
13 The idea is to take on a friend in speculation (10)
15 A few words to the corpse might be harsh punishment (5,8)
19 Attractive expression when accepting a proposal (8,5)
23 Grass – stern correction when you go astray (10)
25 Makes more sound as a tool (4)
28 Got up in some excitement (6)
29 Mad greed and confusion (8)
30 Slow general captured by foreign agent (6)
31 Show the flag as a matter of principle (8)

DOWN

1 Years taken to get the corrupt New Testament removed (6)
2 Give everybody a pained expression (5)
3 Award given after a pound on one's ear (4)
4 Leave dock in second-hand clothes (4-3)
6 Seafood not cooked in empty pan (5)
7 Unhealthy take-away (9)
8 It's a sweet life for one making flower calls (5-3)
11 Punishment is no bad thing (4)
14 Examination assessment not to spoil a top person (4)
15 Making a name as a writer (9)
16 Get depressed with no women and no time (3)
17 A couple need one to make one (4)
18 They make faces when shown articles in the paper (8)
20 Noah's first use of craft to annoy (4)
21 It's thought one might have committed a crime (7)
22 People of some dedication recovered after a break (6)
24 Mary's grown-up follower? (5)
26 Teaching a pet to lead its master (5)
27 Fabric for a grass skirt? (4)

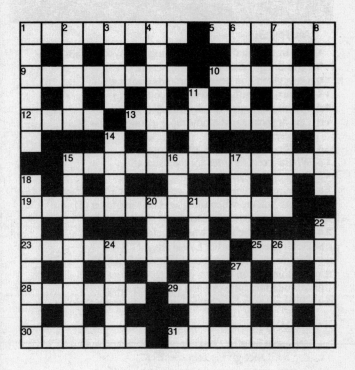

ACROSS

1 Accumulation of errors requiring you to call again (5,6)
9 Firm in repetition identifying a winner (7)
10 Dash when you hear the broth is cooking (7)
11 Animal returning with cub in collapse (3)
12 Person privileged to take liberty (7)
13 One of those same atoms representing a mass of difference (7)
14 Can be found at home after a time (3)
15 Where a regular goes for the usual (5)
17 Proper privilege (5)
18 Require to go in the back way to find things to carry out (5)
20 Where you are when things get on top of you (5)
22 Take possession of a carrier (3)
24 Division of the locks when togetherness ends (7)
25 Don't keep to the diet Eva arranged (7)
26 Serious when loss of home causes a flap (3)
27 Anything taken on by a priest producing tension (7)
28 Admitted by little girl and boy when asked (7)
29 Shifts are sold here by one in a beastly trade (5-6)

DOWN

1 Use air to no effect talking to the unreceptive (5,4,6)
2 Top mail shot giving best results (7)
3 Having no experience of being stopped (5)
4 Amateurish murder in out-of-the-way dunes (9)
5 Room here for a lady certain to drop a point when the port comes up (7)
6 Britain's possession of the hard stuff (4,2,9)
7 In favour of making healthy gains (6)
8 Turn stern perhaps when there's disturbance (6)
16 Runner concealing wish not to drink vegetable offering (9)
18 Blunt warning? (3-3)
19 Lively person having a ball (7)
21 Man with orders to find one girl for a dramatic comeback (7)
23 Note sounding vibrant with desire (6)
25 A lot of whist players approaching the house (5)

20

ACROSS

1 A reflection to make us laugh (7)
5 Crafty turn in an awful state (6)
9 Strange people start to triumph in a scrap (7)
10 One of those that might give you a heavy boot (7)
11 Advertise on the radio (3)
12 A mastermind at work for peace (11)
13 Hunter of the stars (5)
14 Won state backing to be gathered up all round (9)
16 Lying about with Latin inclination (9)
17 Material insertion of a list of names (5)
19 See greed tag as not the right way to bring people together (11)
22 Almost arrived at an eccentric projection (3)
23 Drank a lot when cleaned out (7)
24 Exclusive on an industrial dispute (7)
26 The ass is continuing with the wrong gear (6)
27 Appalled by strong current feeling (7)

DOWN

1 A very old cur going round looking sort of green (7)
2 Being considered inferior talk? (5,10)
3 Anger when the shooting hasn't started (3)
4 They might be opened for some of those looking at estate agents' boards (5)
5 Another BR crash – how awful! (9)
6 Fine portion? Turn it up – it's bone! (5)
7 One that lets you know if you're getting there on time? (10,5)
8 Scheduled to be given a stiff reprimand (6)
12 Material produced from a sudden impulse to reveal all (5)
14 He makes a claim before getting an offer (9)
15 Temptation for Jack to make brandy (5)
16 Beautiful girl artist encountered in our salad days (6)
18 Restricted in a description of the company (7)
20 Paul ends in unspeakable prison camp (5)
21 Mountains of maps (5)
25 Express wonder at the shop where you can get a penny off (3)

ACROSS

1 Ring of blood at home? (6,6)
8 Outlaws angry in addition (7)
9 Urge again to keep in check (7)
11 It's said to distinguish this hobble from others (10)
12 Permissive circle in Ireland (4)
14 Allow support to be given before drink is taken in (8)
16 Not seen greeting dunderhead at the wrong end (6)
17 Missile man (3)
19 Back works employment for partner (6)
21 Another move to get some feedback (8)
24 Promising to tell the truth, one takes it (4)
25 Cons umpire craftily in a bit of theatre (10)
27 Point to great quantities of pasta (7)
28 A setback for the setter causing heated state (7)
29 Movement of monster crane bringing strong protest (12)

DOWN

1 A long way to go before Chinese pottery can represent cultivation (7)
2 Personal chemistry transforms the mimosa belt (10)
3 Too apathetic to carry a catalogue (8)
4 Pay taken by copper to assist the vicar (6)
5 Line taken by all European currencies (4)
6 Pull fish up while going with the wind (7)
7 One of 12 used with stirring effect (7,5)
10 Cursed at having to fight each other? (5,7)
13 Choice showing good sense (10)
15 One might be lent to a speaker (3)
18 Chaps curse what they have to put on (8)
20 Result of an extraction (7)
22 Be like one friend who has taken it in (7)
23 Moment of truth when credit is repeated (6)
26 A lot of upheaval in the choir (4)

ACROSS

6 Something else to do with cooking chips? (5,4,2,3)
9 Bordering on the unconventional (6)
10 Bureaucrat language (8)
11 Wrong rate sorted out after some obscurity (8)
13 Genuine protection for practitioner back in the food store (6)
15 Bigger bills expected when one keeps a pet inside (6)
17 Tutor about to tease a fearsome creature (6)
19 Number to put in the vessel if you want it strong (6)
20 Points to paper ring needed for coffee (8)
22 Scarlet flounces around the piano in ghostly form (8)
24 Soothsayer able to make nothing clear perhaps (6)
26 Await events in order to be a witness (3,4,7)

DOWN

1 Two future union members maybe (8,6)
2 Not quite the object of successful dieting (4)
3 Stop moving and you'll get very cold (6)
4 Manage to stay in credit as a dealer (8)
5 Painter of movement agreeing to turn up (4)
7 After admission a friend might become a prisoner (6)
8 Pick up a mirror with a wish for good health (5,4,5)
12 More than one plucked out of the ether (5)
14 Conman with Irish accent headed off (5)
16 Take a break to liven art movement (8)
18 Friendly proposal by a drinker (6)
21 Be quick to supply the missing word (6)
23 Cover an animal taken to the pound (4)
25 Make an animal cross at some point (4)

23

ACROSS

1 Not being conscious of deficiency in a fight (8)
5 Aircraftman thrown overboard in a storm (6)
9 Quite happy about commercial song (8)
10 Keeps striking for money (6)
12 There may be a storm after this (4)
13 Think how to cancel freedom (10)
15 Cakes in the Queen's service (5,2,6)
19 Might be said on meeting again years after retiring as bishop (4,4,2,3)
23 Good place to watch a superb defence (10)
25 Hit the bald head of a gentle creature (4)
28 No gore being spilt here in America (6)
29 Make an end of what's distinctive about the pound (8)
30 Len's crazy about girl players (6)
31 One you might play on the other side (8)

DOWN

1 Stir caused by old skirt expander (6)
2 Time to keep quiet in rail crash (5)
3 Showing some sort of consideration (4)
4 Take off an ordinary uniform (7)
6 Eat into royalty on poetry (5)
7 Perform opera badly in Asia (9)
8 Received in error from her maids' carelessness (8)
11 Turn it up very loud and there'll be a row (4)
14 It helps one to enjoy the high life (4)
15 Name Agnes set in metal (9)
16 Have an obligation to take part in the Battle of Flowers (3)
17 Expel for being away with the second intake (4)
18 Means of achieving a standard hold-up (8)
20 Little chap of sound strength (4)
21 Refuse points when it's best to, going on and on (7)
22 Jack having been dispatched elsewhere (6)
24 He's learned that a person isn't a worker (5)
26 Make a case for a royal guest – no way! (5)
27 Start without first Yorkshire pudding (4)

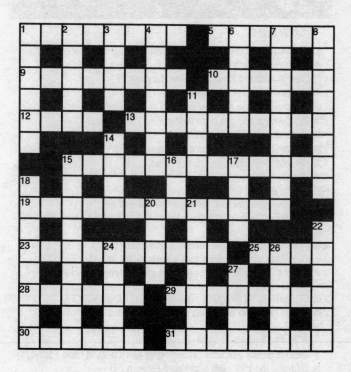

24

ACROSS

1 Thinking the end of the war would bring no worries (5,2,4)
9 Person taking a holiday in the fall? (7)
10 Don't vote for Jack the flawed saint (7)
11 Record unfinished game return (3)
12 He'll find time for a peer's son in any circumstances (7)
13 Encourage the top man to become intellectual (7)
14 Note the carrier's return (3)
15 No problem left for the art supporter (5)
17 People Bert arranged to take one in (5)
18 Parker's time recorder (5)
20 Game played by correspondence? (5)
22 Container sent back as a gift for the talker (3)
24 Party wit uncertain what to say when a titled lady appears (7)
25 Fool maybe, but the fellow's got cover (7)
26 One gets even when a girl's gone sick (3)
27 Where one experiences the ups and downs of modern travel (7)
28 Complaint of people twisting the tail around (7)
29 Hasty old man disposed to become a poet (5,6)

DOWN

1 Depict urban Socialist as going to have a wild time (5,3,4,3)
2 Uphold the old man and show esteem (7)
3 Before one's time (5)
4 Music-maker disturbing the eagle loft (9)
5 Understanding can be seen (7)
6 Sounds of encouragement people don't hear? (9,6)
7 Good man finding foreign money on the beach (6)
8 Nervous at being so near the fall (2,4)
16 Helpful person when wretched Irma is in the grip of the devil (9)
18 Crazy Abyssinian prince in port (6)
19 Tease pretty girl for being a plaything (3-4)
21 Gangster taking cover before a bit gets quietly knocked off (7)
23 Graduates turn out to be African (6)
25 Quarrel about taking the whip (5)

25

ACROSS

1 Linen for a morning on the railway – one among hundreds (7)
5 Express pain on a visit by the young (6)
9 Best choose one for the old lady (7)
10 Can rule out some sort of fission (7)
11 Big loss of gravity in the shade (3)
12 Some loss of face when a Conservative accepts help from an employee (7,4)
13 Strip and lisp a number (5)
14 Violent mixing of our ices (9)
16 Prone to treat sport as requiring speed (9)
17 Conscious of having a following at sea (5)
19 The colour behind one's touch (4-7)
22 Strange heart of an Enid Blyton character (3)
23 Impression of literature (7)
24 It's an achievement to find the lady something of a flier (7)
26 Be an inseparable part of where we are now (6)
27 No longer working when repeatedly exhausted (7)

DOWN

1 Little reptile tangling the lace (7)
2 View stuff possibly not agreed (6,2,7)
3 Odd place for discussing Foreign Office departure (3)
4 Funny business taking a bit of the mickey (5)
5 Where to meet the crowd (9)
6 Fortunate monarch to be embraced by a lady (5)
7 Somehow offering a choice of routes (3,3,2,7)
8 Ring them when they attend union gatherings (6)
12 Struggle to make a getaway without a pound (5)
14 Bouquet for student fundraising in the country (9)
15 Train, or just part of one (5)
16 Think about keeping quiet over revolutionary rising (6)
18 Submitted to rude misbehaviour in the last resort (7)
20 There's nothing evil around you can put into words (5)
21 Conclude a friend to be not entirely put out (5)
25 Inclined to make a point shortly (3)

ACROSS

1 Bemused chum has to place a bet in a short time getting it wrong (4,8)
8 Fall in the winter while failing to gain a coach (7)
9 Set aside one to receive sound man (7)
11 Quiet note in stream being the cause of action (5,5)
12 Pleasing reduction last time (4)
14 Gets Enid in trouble and is taken in (8)
16 Think of a fashionable opening (6)
17 Expert touch (3)
19 Cause tears at school (6)
21 Spoil scripture teaching when it's time for a get-together (8)
24 Lied about not having a job (4)
25 Accepting what will happen if it's a talc that's split (10)
27 It's hard to get excited about the Indian Queen (7)
28 More mad alphabetical extremes included by the man making public announcements (7)
29 Condition achieved by investment (5,2,5)

DOWN

1 Intending to get Nina and Meg involved (7)
2 One isn't the same after this (10)
3 Left isolated in a mood near distraction (8)
4 One looks to do a stretch in faultless service (6)
5 Offhand delivery of first-class line (4)
6 Mark's removal not in doubt after a time (7)
7 Vessels returning with fruit on the wrong night to get some peace (4,8)
10 Achieve a sporting record without playing (4,3,5)
13 Excessive rain on tide getting rough (10)
15 Injury time deducted for obstruction (3)
18 Doesn't fall for South American city supplying outdated arms (8)
20 Depending on bombast to cover an awful lie (7)
22 Failure to start last outing on a horse (7)
23 Look on board for a way out place to view (6)
26 Sort out by shaking a fist (4)

ACROSS

6 Be bored when conducted round fashionable street rebuilding (4,2,8)
9 Forbid articles of fruit (6)
10 Damage done after cur has run round (8)
11 One runs out of things to wear (8)
13 Refuse to find fault with note while being curious (6)
15 Opportunity to take a gamble (6)
17 Tore in and around the East (6)
19 Weight added to bed cloth (6)
20 Shoot out of the studio here (8)
22 Girl with giant problem not in a fix (8)
24 They take turns to get tight (6)
26 Turn to lie throbbing and cause to get very hot (5,2,3,4)

DOWN

1 Great wave of posh travel between Ireland and America? (8,6)
2 Bird getting stuck in a joint, say (4)
3 Dispose of possessions on arrival (6)
4 Leaves out its use during an outpouring (8)
5 Youngster starting to riot in strike (4)
7 Not well employed by the company (6)
8 Shakespeare's effectiveness in showing determination (8,2,4)
12 Right according to former law (5)
14 Exhausted by all that shopping? (5)
16 Succeeds in prosecuting people inside (8)
18 Hurried retreat by local leader in conflict (6)
21 We come up with the money required by some nut (6)
23 You can see her going up and down (4)
25 Opening up a quarter of an acre (4)

ACROSS

1 Display fine feathers in a confrontation (8)
5 Prevent what possibly leads to extremes of resentment (6)
9 It gives an impression of dispatch (8)
10 See difficulty getting round the course to pass (6)
12 Not alive to the need for good time-keeping (4)
13 Driver crashing in the Rio race (10)
15 Very latest report of print strike (4-5,4)
19 How progress can be made when normal circulation is blocked (5,3,5)
23 Stop in the subway to get the message (10)
25 Watch out for an opening (4)
28 Silent preparation to become a soldier (6)
29 take no notice of something knocked off (8)
30 Old rulers of the union taking one from a girl (6)
31 A riot tag may apply to a forceful speaker (8)

DOWN

1 Drink and work for what one may receive (6)
2 Attach levelled against the group (5)
3 Leave in some awful place (4)
4 Display great respect for his address as mayor (7)
6 He will shortly get round to offering a greeting (5)
7 Fear to make an arrest (9)
8 Speculate about the zero pay increase (8)
11 Fact acknowledged by the faithful (4)
14 Give a performance otherwise one may be closed (4)
15 Cuddle she might have planned (9)
16 He might let you see the light (3)
17 Raised to such an extent as to give diners a start (4)
18 Reminder of the brief time people are protected by teachers (8)
20 Expressing opposition in Greek and Roman times (4)
21 Giving performances without cease (7)
22 Guide soldiers to high position (6)
24 One of those that take you up on a flight (5)
26 Mature announcement made last month (5)
27 Brer Rabbit's last appearance (4)

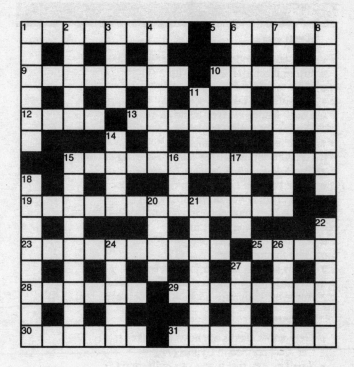

ACROSS

1 Assistance needed to get out of Highland pen (7,4)
9 Bribes those who are not with it (7)
10 Time to be found in zero credit (7)
11 Measure turn taken by a bird (3)
12 Chuck having escaped being an exile (7)
13 Unpleasant refusal to give one an unspecified amount (7)
14 No time for school at this age (3)
15 Having seen the bill the fellow is feeling uncomfortable (5)
17 Come down where you can be seen (5)
18 Show you don't care for quiet cover (5)
20 Top person laying down the line (5)
22 Request last-moment removal from the job (3)
24 Allow an escape to get flat (7)
25 It's a tan of sorts that one gains (7)
26 Time to drop the sea issue (3)
27 Life is starting here for foreigners (7)
28 Printing what's serious about the old place (7)
29 Bottle institution from which control is exercised (5-6)

DOWN

1 Memorable chorus of ghosts on strike? (8,7)
2 Car Alan crashed in Cyprus (7)
3 Small picture that is part of a collection (5)
4 Growing reasons for taking on the Spanish (9)
5 Rising provision of workers' accommodation (3-4)
6 Advance to be returned with thanks (4,2,9)
7 Has to move mineral off the ship (6)
8 One's not allowed to go under it (6)
16 It's lucky one's on the hoof (9)
18 A cruel one's said to worry a good person (6)
19 Take note when idler is the one to provide a glass (7)
21 Take it back when the carrier turns up on time (7)
23 Fate encountered after a ski mishap (6)
25 Try to corner a swimmer? (5)

ACROSS

1 Monsieur Osbert reforms one of the gang (7)
5 Time to show flexibility (6)
9 One has visions of a ram mingling with deer (7)
10 Not well placed here in Calais when being at the tunnel opening isn't allowed (7)
11 It contributes some fluidity in writing of a certain kind (3)
12 Fine – nice fit maybe but not working very well (11)
13 Shane has turned quite pale! (5)
14 Marked by varied fortunes when payment is followed by debt (9)
16 People of note (9)
17 Fear about being caught by the old man (5)
19 Feels uncertain about five hundred on the perimeter offering resistance (4-7)
22 Vessel with potential (3)
23 It shows where we might get a drink (3,4)
24 Trace underwear one has to take back for instance (7)
26 There's money to be made by dodging the law (6)
27 State who left the complete embargo in force (7)

DOWN

1 Forced Republicans to have a drink (7)
2 Create a shattering row (5,3,7)
3 Man with German upbringing (3)
4 Unusual energy for such a small show (5)
5 Not being at ease might make Tess sniff (9)
6 Survival of Jewish priest given Catholic protection (5)
7 Source of energy for big bomb retaliation (7,8)
8 Said to be at Ted's disposal (6)
12 Style of perfection ice skaters may show (5)
14 Take teasing a little further and get the bird (9)
15 Excessive subscription required by an international body (5)
16 Secret punishment I have not completed (6)
18 Try to get paid for having gone around the prison (7)
20 Go through coach (5)
21 Book a man for concealing vice at first (5)
25 Be sorry the top man doesn't quite get a rise (3)

31

ACROSS

1 Amusing take-off? (5,7)
8 Champion person known to be good in an extremity (7)
9 Thought to have grass placed inside (7)
11 It could be a novel responsibility (10)
12 Warning laugh (4)
14 Slow progress having no sound effect (8)
16 One might be needed by a bridge trio (6)
17 Make a hit that could be a turn-on (3)
19 Invention of a figure (6)
21 Soup and chop when getting involved with Gaza (8)
24 Nip quietly away for a measure (4)
25 Came round with animal to Elmer's End as one carrying authority (4-6)
27 Foot runner (7)
28 Trying to get fools included on the way back (7)
29 Lent one for a time (3,9)

DOWN

1 Work out the cost of having to secure a dog (7)
2 Looking back could be rot in a sense (10)
3 Nice requests by a little one (8)
4 Far-off help offered for the fearful (6)
5 Give impressions of characters (4)
6 Not covered for absence at the opening (7)
7 No falling-off in suitable intake? (8,4)
10 Bottle after bottle (5,7)
13 MEPs scored badly when the squeeze was on (10)
15 There's nothing to be said for applying it (3)
18 One's thought of something new to get butter right out of a dish (8)
20 Corrupt man with financial obligations (7)
22 Guarantee ref is involved with City corruption (7)
23 Not allowed to sound like a poet (6)
26 Put away from point to point (4)

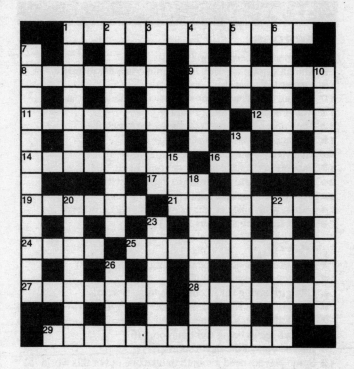

ACROSS

6 Not there by permission (5,2,7)
9 More room for the lady to accommodate her former partner (6)
10 Getting too much on top of the accommodation one is in (8)
11 Bill gets firm new deal award (8)
13 They take clothes for wearing on the beach (6)
15 Go back and do the twist again (6)
17 Take away the little man in the passage (6)
19 Expert ran into setback for the time being (3,3)
20 One has a scornful attitude to Parliamentarians (8)
22 Urge to become an apostle (8)
24 Hair-raising place of imprisonment? (4-2)
26 Don't stay to read letters (6,4,4)

DOWN

1 One's firing is not as fatal as it might sound (5,9)
2 Goodbye to depression (4)
3 City girl having the intelligence to go first (6)
4 Has a set been shuffled when one wasn't there? (8)
5 Don't abandon a stronghold (4)
7 Girl we see as being right in bloom (6)
8 Ins and outs of the day's sport (7,7)
12 Some players need a month to take one out of this world (5)
14 Normal American superior to Los Angeles upstarts (5)
16 Run into sections that protect defenders (8)
18 Hide an Indian among Poles (6)
21 The case for putting some lilies in a pot (6)
23 Letting all compete round the enclosure (4)
25 Quite relaxed when there's no fire maybe (4)

ACROSS

1 For instance one dropped into the cider brew could be a killer (8)
5 One of the cast could be making notes (6)
9 Swimmer taking endless wine with dignity (8)
10 Dislike colour on the cover (6)
12 One of those taken in advance (4)
13 Indulges in dreams as a fitness exercise (10)
15 Good support needed with the powerful in retreat (6,7)
19 You know where you are when you can see the pub (5,8)
23 Getting ready for working as a doctor (10)
25 Ruler finding a way to show the Queen round (4)
28 Bankrupt one under difficulty all round (6)
29 Time to make another date (8)
30 Talk about tiny feet on the go! (6)
31 Deduction for containers returned by an attendant (8)

DOWN

1 Take it easy – put the question again (6)
2 It's always green in spring or September (5)
3 Exult in being able to fly direct (4)
4 Scorn what might be said in a row (7)
6 Shows the way to get on a flat roof (5)
7 Standard measures taken to get credit (9)
8 Give new shape to a flag that lacks a point (8)
11 Doubts arise after smoking (4)
14 Said to be bad but for one small measure (4)
15 One left as it coils around (9)
16 One might go off and cause death (3)
17 Nice porcelain missing – must be the cleaner! (4)
18 Role played by friend caught up in flashy display (8)
20 Taking part in a national song contest, what's more! (4)
21 You may be open-mouthed to meet him at work (7)
22 Given an order he will squirm with discomfort (6)
24 That's the place for soothing repetition (5)
26 Hot rock publication by somebody learned (5)
27 Break for photography (4)

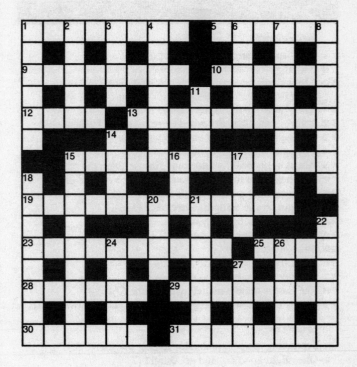

34

ACROSS

1 Dirty and possibly cruel pay-off (6,5)
9 Backing strike with clever story (7)
10 Cheat skinhead to triumph – it's easily done without a rum (7)
11 Everything possessed by a Bible man (3)
12 Tells of real difficulty when there's a setback (7)
13 Not happy to be living on handouts? (7)
14 Example of rotundity and conceit (3)
15 About to get healthy and ready for use again (5)
17 Finish the crossword and you begin to be a smart one (5)
18 Warning from a dealer to his customers (5)
20 It might be one's alternative choice (5)
22 He's held dear by many a writer (3)
24 Bovine error seen as a bloomer (7)
25 Strange little scrap (7)
26 Beast responsible for Bert's carry-on (3)
27 Left one by the business entrance (7)
28 The East is mine – including the name (7)
29 Happy condition of being drunk before getting down (4,7)

DOWN

1 Promoting top personal value as best one can (3,3,4,5)
2 One might go to pot and get caught (7)
3 Rotters but one takes to them when a quick getaway is wanted (5)
4 Final depression where no further retreat is possible (4,5)
5 Went cold at seeing an infant swallow a piece of lead (7)
6 Desperate situation when the tie-up can't be extended (3,2,4,6)
7 Scattered boxes at the top of Everest (6)
8 Another chance to see action in connection with drama (6)
16 Evidence given by stupid person proving infallible (9)
18 Reply favourably to what's proposed (6)
19 Decisive in a sneaky sort of way? (7)
21 Plate of beetroot having a colourful inclination? (7)
23 Go round and see rubbish consumed (6)
25 Last character to appear in a winning home game twice (5)

35

ACROSS

1 Be left with a month's first sound measure (7)
5 Say what you have learned (6)
9 Reasons for going round a stately home (7)
10 Holiday accommodation for Vera and Nat abroad (7)
11 Money returned without material assistance (3)
12 Celebrity division (11)
13 Adding a flavour of insolence (5)
14 Not still in a state of fear (9)
16 State when take-off has been completed (9)
17 Still seen as among the finer tennis players of the century (5)
19 Favouring parts of relative magnitude (11)
22 Pop group engagement to get people going? (3)
23 Fancy I need a drink inside me (7)
24 Day I consumed enough to give complete gratification (7)
26 Turn attention to making a short announcement (6)
27 Invest a couple of hundred in a girl who can bring the ship good fortune (7)

DOWN

1 Follow quotations that establish identity (3,4)
2 Dream situation in the sky when the mad have to come down (5-6-4)
3 Hair style that looks good enough to eat (3)
4 Less worried about the round one fails to win (5)
5 What one pays to keep servants? (9)
6 After a century one man is representative of the community (5)
7 Move to express shock after death (4,2,4,5)
8 Pictures one in underwear (6)
12 Fear it might be the last word you take in (5)
14 Throw rotten meat into the river as ordered by the doctor (9)
15 Gets together without English military groups (5)
16 Overturn cooking utensil and the family will provide something to wipe it up (6)
18 Hardy heroine holding rig-out that makes her a fierce one (7)
20 Nothing to survive on but fruit (5)
21 Rest here perhaps with circulation in present form (5)
25 Involuntary movement of the captain's heart when in charge (3)

36

ACROSS

1 Worry about when to leave a business that's still trading (5,7)
8 Music man with some art at his disposal (7)
9 Recruits find a way into broken lines (7)
11 Provokes the clever without being required to (10)
12 Skirt an Italian resort offering no religious instruction (4)
14 Quick Frenchman's return producing something of a fix (8)
16 Old instrument fixer ready to come round (6)
17 Fool in a trench (3)
19 Admitted having a friend in an institution (6)
21 Casual worker said not to be religious (8)
24 Annoy someone who'll tell the police (4)
25 Nine mature characters unable to understand mathematics (10)
27 Maybe as cruel but not as religious (7)
28 Break the tin, find the drink and get weaving (7)
29 The mischief animals get up to (6-6)

DOWN

1 Old men invest almost nothing in horses (7)
2 Let clients make up their minds (10)
3 Examples of smooth and shining journalism (8)
4 Just about to take exercises without concealment (6)
5 Cry out for a visit (4)
6 European rains storming around America (7)
7 In pleasant company at a meeting-house maybe (5,7)
10 When outer protection is removed they still conceal arms (5-7)
13 Furious article, outburst on Celtic dancing (10)
15 Sooner leave her and run away (3)
18 Funny not to get laughs (8)
20 State of the leather (7)
22 They find pop groups a moving experience but turn aside after roughness starts (7)
23 Drive Green crazy at the end of the day (6)
26 Heavy criticism of careless cake-watcher turning up without embarrassment (4)

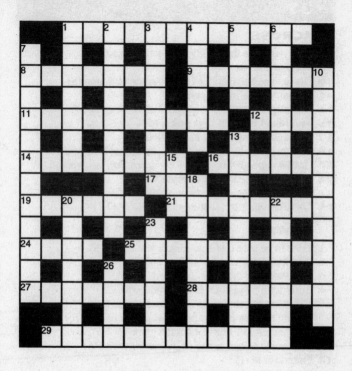

37

ACROSS

6 They've made the family connection (7,3,4)
9 Mind you be there (6)
10 One comes between 6 to make romantic drama (8)
11 Intensify the hinge fracture (8)
13 One might have to be weighed before departure (6)
15 Fish round the river depression (6)
17 Average means of communication (6)
19 One might go in and out to get something moving (6)
20 Can be depended on to give ear when libel is involved (8)
22 Heading for Scots seat of royalty (8)
24 Same again please for the traveller to take in (6)
26 There couldn't be a better one to follow (7,7)

DOWN

1 Time to be sure one's no longer young (4,7,3)
2 Carl leaves the city for a bit of land (4)
3 Robber group that's on to something (6)
4 Bully with no instinct to be a buddy (8)
5 Move around aimlessly like a bird (4)
7 Loving to see a pet swallow a whole lot of food (6)
8 One has a lot of imitators in the game (6-2-6)
12 One's entertained to see us get embarrassed (5)
14 Friend for tea (5)
16 Study the leaflet that offers a deal (8)
18 Young swimmer starting early to follow wayward girls (6)
21 A trial is rigged – so it's the rope! (6)
23 Miss a means of keeping hands warm (4)
25 Means of conveying liquid smoke? (4)

38

ACROSS

1 Sounding superior, what a troublesome chief! (8)
5 Hits out at bad beer (6)
9 Overseas driving facilitator (3,5)
10 Pat's achievement (6)
12 Weapon for fluid warfare (4)
13 The one you love here at West Wittering (10)
15 It tells you what will happen if the attack doesn't get cold (7,6)
19 Domestic office help for the minister (4,9)
23 Curious lid made to look absurd (10)
25 One's worried about the teacher heading the school (4)
28 Remove hair and make free (6)
29 Girl clever enough to go round looking sweet (8)
30 Catch a hot pipe (6)
31 Liberated to triumph without one in West Africa (8)

DOWN

1 Underworld character one doesn't like to see going round the City (6)
2 Cover article giving expert protection (5)
3 In a rebuilt plane we can fly once more (4)
4 Laugh to drown uneasiness at what's obtained with difficulty (4-3)
6 Look at the time! (5)
7 Any profit distribution may be subject to abuse (9)
8 Put away in case (8)
11 Accept there's no trick and give up (4)
14 Classical bird, this girl! (4)
15 Crazy to plunge into a stream to get round an animal (9)
16 Low creature unable to complete the treatment (3)
17 Going around with a friend can be precious (4)
18 Comprehensive reform of the hot and violent (8)
20 Shout when both sides have scored a hundred (4)
21 European money takes the wrong road in South America (7)
22 Not prepared to be translated (6)
24 Firm repetition over a drink (5)
26 Forbidden to show appreciation so do the other thing! (5)
27 Finally right to regret what can't be denied (4)

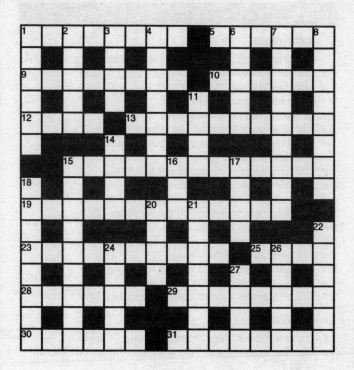

39

ACROSS

1 Naked as lace is abandoned for the good things of life (5,3,3)
9 Animal attendant in a frenzy (7)
10 Liable to have an affair (7)
11 Crazy one's turn to get tight (3)
12 Dismissed and maybe left in the street (7)
13 Bad to damage memorial and remove engraved head (7)
14 So far the snowman can do without one (3)
15 Be quick to make it (5)
17 Creatures going north and possibly west (5)
18 Put on a talk without commercial (5)
20 The walk that shows one's in drink (5)
22 Struggle not to get heated on the way back (3)
24 Show fear when there's a quake (7)
25 Tempting creature before going back in to be dispatched (7)
26 Ready for all of them! (3)
27 Awkward to get away in a leaderless group (7)
28 Well-known nine met trouble here! (7)
29 Talk of a getaway could lead to an explosion (8,3)

DOWN

1 Arrive to get a savings movement going (4,2,3,6)
2 Like the tricks of those from whom the Queen needs to be saved (7)
3 The row that's part of an act? (5)
4 Tennis ass involved in something unpleasant (9)
5 Something in the egg turning man blue (7)
6 It takes pluck to use them over personal vision (7,8)
7 It's the place of religion to take it out of superior importance (6)
8 Fails to continue progress in the theatre (6)
16 Plenty of room in it for long-distance travel? (9)
18 Turn Red out to go the long way round (6)
19 Fuss cub might make of academic dress (7)
21 Making a mistake about a personal adornment (7)
23 Go around or up over the gallery (6)
25 Grim conclusion (5)

40

ACROSS

1 Indicated the way to be sharp (7)
5 Church get-up in red (6)
9 State of a fashionable princess (7)
10 Lively support in oral composition (7)
11 Unfinished craft in fur or feathers (3)
12 Shabby plaid one takes to be out of fashion (11)
13 One flies to get some of the detergent back (5)
14 Academic to employ heartless lady in a generous way (9)
16 A resort to fun with American food item (9)
17 Richard, the singer who gives us rock (5)
19 Convert one born here to something different (11)
22 One might get carried away by one pop performance (3)
23 One appears in various titles as a supporter of superiority (7)
24 Graceful ends achieved by romance and charm (7)
26 What's heavenly about the pub is not the stout (6)
27 Got to the point of recording a warning of danger (7)

DOWN

1 Quietly inclined to be easily led (7)
2 Asian going up the line without support can be an illusion (6,4-5)
3 It's refreshing not to start late for a change (3)
4 Learned man becoming something of a bore in slow speech (5)
5 They're the best plants you can have around the hospital (9)
6 Made a decision to go straight (5)
7 Holiday people going round having visions (11,4)
8 Doctor Andy having trouble early in the week (6)
12 Put off the cleaner when the fellow's gone (5)
14 Pray agent is able to organise display (9)
15 Relative's dirty article suppressed (5)
16 Declined to be at the centre of a resting place (6)
18 Having designs being worked out (7)
20 Have a royal time in the shower, so to speak (5)
21 Gained admission to the bar? (5)
25 When needing a little money one put the bite on Cleo (3)

41

ACROSS

1 No voting here, it's an absolute rule (12)
8 They may be put out for making contact (7)
9 Succeed in getting boots away from feet maybe (4,3)
11 A ruling art possibly having some points (10)
12 Last thing you'd expect of a peaceful person? (4)
14 Joins on to foreign nobleman sent wandering around (8)
16 Broadcaster regarded as one of the family (6)
17 Animal needed to provide for future growth (3)
19 Use cod as a form of currency (6)
21 Brutal refusal to admit graduate could get almost wealthy (8)
24 A hot turn of speech (4)
25 One sees the future use of force as a bloomer (10)
27 Lecture a month until new mail is delivered (7)
28 Strips in front of the window (7)
29 Further education after a starter (6,6)

DOWN

1 I'd get in difficulty governing the intake (7)
2 Employees not responsible for doing the dirty (5,5)
3 Attacks the fool with a raging lust (8)
4 Annie for instance might perform on harp (6)
5 Disposed of what began to be seen as outdated (4)
6 It's hard at first to be the one to mock (7)
7 Not quite the best yet in confidence (3,3,6)
10 Total cover provided at the lowest level (6,6)
13 Stupid attendant left holding the food (4-6)
15 Show distress this way at not getting top mark (3)
18 Defeat later overturned in court (8)
20 Dead skin reduced to baffle lice (7)
22 Way to leave a sinking ship? Take a step in the rigging (7)
23 Fated to perform when there's nothing but sea to be seen (6)
26 Game to go the long way round (4)

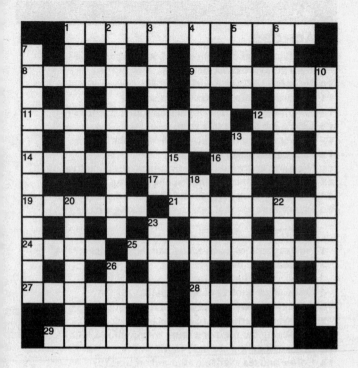

42

ACROSS

6 Not fair to make selling one's house unprofitable? (8,6)
9 Burden said to cause delay (6)
10 He paints badly as a performer (8)
11 One values animals, the tailless sort (8)
13 Regulating the action of old China after it returns (6)
15 Give a job by way of a gesture (6)
17 Flower of America following a swimmer (6)
19 Heavenly streaker (6)
20 Weapons appear to cause anger in places of cultivation (8)
22 Name oils that can be mixed in a pudding (8)
24 Close to getting caught inside having a drink (6)
26 Part of the crew that bars coward making a move (9,5)

DOWN

1 No exaggeration in an account of the depression? (14)
2 Excited move into silver (4)
3 Eastern departure for figure of eminence (6)
4 One finds it a job to pick a team (8)
5 Second escape from collapse of the mass (4)
7 One who is dedicated to the electoral process? (6)
8 Answering the need of a drink with comfort (3,3,8)
12 Make certain it's not right to follow (5)
14 Coffee and tea available after a short time (5)
16 Ring Rosa to go round and see where the soldiers are (8)
18 Business romance (6)
21 About this time Nelson started to achieve fame (6)
23 What we have the French bear (4)
25 The truth is Vera's lost the place (4)

43

ACROSS

1 Such an onslaught can be a bit dire (8)
5 The outlaw gang is on to something (6)
9 Strong defence in respect of hair (8)
10 Same characters maybe – but that's another story! (6)
12 On your head be it, brother! (4)
13 You're a long way down the line from him (10)
15 Useful contact in the royal circle (6,2,5)
19 In a position to ask a favour without having full standing (2,6,5)
23 Gifts she'll have distributed without being able to take off (10)
25 Former top person in a tyrant's army (4)
28 Inclined to emphasise something one's reading (6)
29 Our dream might be to be given protection (8)
30 Attempt to get round what a consumer will do to get agreement (6)
31 Egregious bombast about national display (8)

DOWN

1 Spoil fish by including a bit of beef (6)
2 It shows the way to go when a school lacks aspiration (5)
3 Unusual copper leaving poison (4)
4 What to play shortly before graduation day? (7)
6 A thousand and one defections from a country where there may be fighting (5)
7 Tug hounds around to find things to eat (9)
8 Don't mind having to carry a real mess inside (8)
11 Make the girl a goddess (4)
14 Roaring success as a celebrity? (4)
15 Invent a building block that has to be shortened in the end (9)
16 Turn into divine incompetent (3)
17 Get jaw going and find a lot to cut (4)
18 Combat trick used by French policeman to end a riot (8)
20 She goes on a bit of a bender with Pat (4)
21 One preys on small creatures among one's weakest relatives (7)
22 Honour an obligation to pay later (6)
24 Raise one among many (5)
26 Land fresh rise to add to initial salary (5)
27 Yearn for an extension (4)

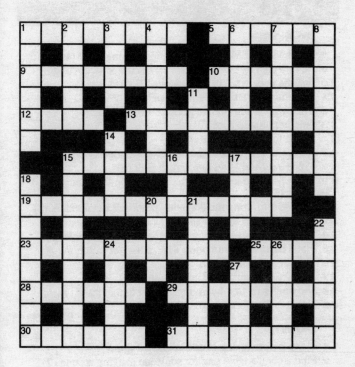

44

ACROSS

1 Not having the slightest inclination to run away? (4,7)
9 Be reflected by having only a small edition in circulation (7)
10 Just the person to get a ball going (7)
11 Something of a theatregoer's vanity (3)
12 Chap with inappropriate gear for an executive (7)
13 Find her tuna to cook (7)
14 Polish food not the starter (3)
15 Not quite shut back at the hotel, your highness (5)
17 Voice a refusal to go in to finish later (5)
18 Projection of one's own personality to protect Hungarian leader (5)
20 Little girl offering the odd ode for home entertainment (5)
22 Where you can turn up and find a head on the beer (3)
24 Not that famous mad nun taking in royalty this time (7)
25 Made harmless commotion when cut short in action (7)
26 The car's motor appears cold . . . (3)
27 . . . very cold during a Gallic outing (7)
28 Showing affection by giving support to the head? (7)
29 Noted rather peculiar solid figure (11)

DOWN

1 Lying before taking in and taking off (3,3,9)
2 Find a comfortable seat for someone hanging around (7)
3 Down there in Australia (5)
4 Improved the picture by further fingering (9)
5 Clothing item a German's thrown out – it's got one missing (7)
6 Immense enthusiasm for high-rise building? (8,7)
7 Resort to including capital in credit (6)
8 As a novelist one looks for missing directions (6)
16 Writing of early days might make Julie vain (9)
18 Make one's mark as a bad writer (6)
19 List for distribution by one whose trade may be blooming (7)
21 Person of rank to clear the rink? (7)
23 Where to buy drink for a person when time's up (6)
25 Too stupid to be spaced out (5)

45

ACROSS

1 Resolves to go from last month to the middle of March (7)
5 Mother is given issue of fruit (6)
9 Managed to go back with half the study group (7)
10 The part that gets men in a tizzy (7)
11 Fuss about our time circle (3)
12 Scolding chap for rule breaking (11)
13 Approved among a number giving evidence (5)
14 Novice given the go-ahead on an instrument (9)
16 Do Red Army manoeuvre in desert transport (9)
17 In Georgia there's a very small measure of radiation (5)
19 It enables you to see the bigger picture (11)
22 Shelter put back for a swimmer (3)
23 Think about cancelling a letter to restore harmony (7)
24 Get the last of these out of the way in a holiday area (7)
26 You won't be so foolish when you come to yours (6)
27 Abridged edition returned with moderate pleasure (7)

DOWN

1 Comment on the impression made about bills arising (7)
2 We're all aware of the ground we share (6,9)
3 Man to put on (3)
4 The bit you have to throw away (5)
5 Dance party to a great extent something new (9)
6 Wonderful Scot capturing a soldier (5)
7 Extra gathering to discuss the flood? (8,7)
8 Taken by the way Noel dances (6)
12 As far as you can get into the mountains (5)
14 Awkward not to give thanks for food (9)
15 Time to put on a cap for a last drink (5)
16 Turn red when you see a girl looking vague (6)
18 Wag tail when people come in to make a complaint (7)
20 Wanders like animals round the ring (5)
21 Stopped without starting to get relaxed (5)
25 One goes through with a determination to throw out the Italian (3)

46

ACROSS

1 No use being famous for being boastful (12)
8 White fur means little to the returning clergyman (7)
9 Tied up in the supporting structure (7)
11 Dropping a division in connection with a diplomatic mission (10)
12 Endless amusement on a ship in a storm (4)
14 Burning to make a cleaner call (8)
16 Easily hurt by an offer (6)
17 Face the other way when it's sticky (3)
19 Departed in non-standard party number (6)
21 Manoeuvre a way in after a Russian retreat (8)
24 Roy's worried about starting great revelry (4)
25 Neutralise the tally at a royal performance (10)
27 Stop somewhere along the line (7)
28 Jet cart adapted to get across (7)
29 Odd behaviour in a strange Syrian disco at the end of the day (12)

DOWN

1 Sort of ice-cream carrier with which one takes everything up (7)
2 Given to air moves that provide extra strength (10)
3 Sailor following non-U person going round (8)
4 Choice of duck with tip on cooking (6)
5 One has to retreat over the border into Spain (4)
6 Not in order if you can't hear it? (7)
7 Curses I can't promise will make a difference (12)
10 Force out of China and make uncertain which way to go? (12)
13 Things wanted by the team in a trade-off (10)
15 Started not to be a killer (3)
18 Something uncanny about lace being so attractive (8)
20 Test team applying new gen to the estate (7)
22 Jack the rebel embraced by a girl in school (7)
23 Gift for suggesting mutiny? (6)
26 Nothing under cover in the pool (4)

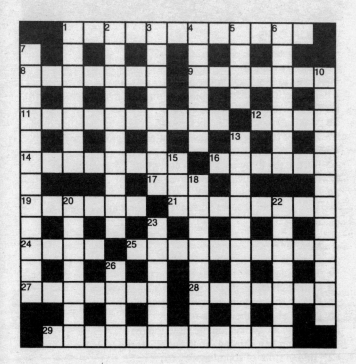

47

ACROSS

6 Star metal in possibly grass etc. (7,7)

9 Country hat (6)

10 Grace to buy tea if going out (8)

11 Tick follower held by notorious marquis in defence work (8)

13 Parted from a fellow in a cap (6)

15 Make allowances for mockery (6)

17 Stagger back bearing vessel of inferior significance (6)

19 Artist back with the others in custody (6)

20 It's got the thing back into a curve that's decorative (8)

22 Deeds run wild when you have parted (8)

24 Get down for a match (6)

26 Talk to some obscure person if you don't know where to write (7,7)

DOWN

1 Obvious what the reason is to remove obstructions (5,3,6)

2 Two aides needed for the old man (4)

3 Chirpy creature, that swine among spies! (6)

4 Hasten to give talk security protection (8)

5 Worry about fancy work (4)

7 Glass globe broken on the table-top (6)

8 Yielding hair shining out in curtain or rug (4,10)

12 Hidden store of sound money (5)

14 They may be taken to bring the possibility of failure (5)

16 One mocks the weekend girl making a theatrical debut (8)

18 Come down and take a turn in the carriage (6)

21 Appreciation for having hot water containers around (6)

23 The obscenity of spiteful gossip (4)

25 One's much admired for getting on having been put in charge (4)

48

ACROSS

1 In truth new life means to give a better appearance (4-4)
5 Favouring the rest being examined (6)
9 Settle in an enclosure (8)
10 Flower of militant womanhood (6)
12 Flattering in order to make things run smoothly? (4)
13 Concerned with the interior set in Latin translation (10)
15 Seek approval to speak freely with leader of the Russian delegation (3,10)
19 No mistakes so far – until now (5,2,2,4)
23 Teacher thinking to become an architect? (10)
25 Red let off as a result of injury (4)
28 One goes around without being on the level (6)
29 Having no qualification Jack therefore takes to a musical instrument (8)
30 Make more profound writer follow the river (6)
31 See lambs skipping to get together (8)

DOWN

1 Fellow performer or agent (6)
2 Arrived and left one with a hump (5)
3 Invitation to observe approved appearance (4)
4 Money can be transferred in a demand for penalty payment (7)
6 Send for terms of reference (5)
7 Any bit involved with Zen can be tortuous (9)
8 Man with good fish on the end of a line (8)
11 Time to go to school (4)
14 Garment not right for burlesque (4)
15 Saintly person spending a month in China maybe (9)
16 Rising hill of rubbish (3)
17 Going gliding without the family causes difficulty (4)
18 Assured more dips might be available (8)
20 Question about the water supply (4)
21 Big volume of passenger movement (7)
22 Get too cold to move (6)
24 Cheer the bishop who has abandoned public relations (5)
26 Not much to eat and drink in honour (5)
27 Emotion may mean nothing (4)

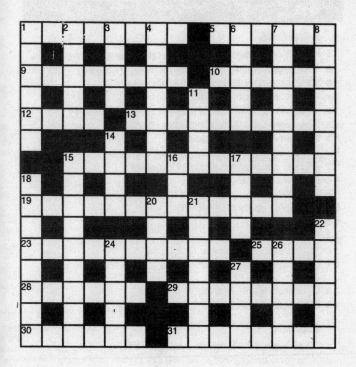

49

ACROSS

1 Lying here with the management providing lodging (3,3,5)
9 Girl Emma endlessly twirling to show sparkle (7)
10 Develop more quickly than indoor plants? (7)
11 Be pictured taking a rest (3)
12 Even having lost heart he can alter and improve (7)
13 It causes a reduction of personal cover (7)
14 Get immersed in depression (3)
15 Show appreciation for the city with no street (5)
17 She has a diet arrangement at the hotel (5)
18 Mutant in play (5)
20 Shout for a beer – not in this low place! (5)
22 Agree one might be sleepy (3)
24 Put in danger of losing a part of a beard (7)
25 Causing damage when in a hurry (7)
26 Flowers worth money in Romania (3)
27 Cod and cake concoction that might be a feather in one's cap (7)
28 Constitute teams as well (7)
29 Members of his band have to be prepared (5-6)

DOWN

1 Good hopes of a future in intelligence (6,9)
2 Nice Mod turning out to be evil (7)
3 Tend to hurry up before the end of the cruise (5)
4 Such love as one may find among trade unionists (9)
5 Like being tried out on horseback (7)
6 Order to one discovering what will tell where waves are coming from (9,6)
7 A great desire to have things settled (6)
8 Squirm to see a shirt-tail on an enchanting female (6)
16 Be superior and get advanced as champion (9)
18 One might be in time to save being one over the eight (6)
19 Storm damaged with some commotion (7)
21 We're on our way in this (7)
23 Take in to understand a strange set (6)
25 You'll find one in a part that stands up in personal support (5)

50

ACROSS

1 One goes in to buy a second jumper . . . (7)
5 . . . a garment with a European look . . . (6)
9 . . . and a good French wrapping to leave behind (7)
10 Anxious to fuel RAF manoeuvres (7)
11 Record the felling of a tree (3)
12 Drink, kiss and transform Erin in verse (11)
13 She's to be found to the west of the Sultanate (5)
14 Roll iron casts out (9)
16 Lays translated in a foreign city have no moving quality (9)
17 Hungrily devour a bird (5)
19 Return the bundle before talking of refinement (11)
22 Complain if one's not included in profit return (3)
23 Points of diversion on the beach (7)
24 Ran round in a confined space killing (7)
26 Break from business in the bay (6)
27 Go back and apply further medication (7)

DOWN

1 Drink in some sort of dive (7)
2 None called me up to provide guns to make a new deal spread (6,9)
3 Where you can hang out a cushion (3)
4 Wash some underwear in sea water (5)
5 Creatures in the nude taking a bitter drug (9)
6 Determination to give support (5)
7 Not starting a place of amusement with something gained by cheating maybe (6,9)
8 One who pays a lawyer has a right to appear in court briefly (6)
12 Make nothing of a girl who goes to unusual extremes (5)
14 They might click for a dance (9)
15 One might be tempted by her warning (5)
16 Content with a quiet time in occupation (6)
18 You can show it without doing anything (7)
20 Like animals of another sort headed off (5)
21 Contract in uncertain currency deal (5)
25 Depression at the heart of reality (3)

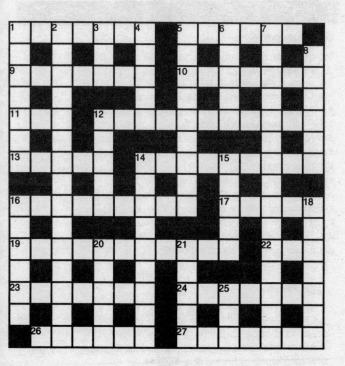

51

ACROSS

1 Funny story having some connection with the family fortune (4,8)
8 Draw a wagon back into the race (7)
9 Little time needed to compile records (7)
11 Able to communicate thought of cheap title transfer (10)
12 Dead animal in the drink (4)
14 Showed lack of concern to shut up the rude (8)
16 Bear back at an American city seen as fair game (4-2)
17 Expert touch (3)
19 Transport youngster in a big bottle (6)
21 Member in the early years of a great resort (8)
24 Excess of gravity in the story – no way! (4)
25 They are able to keep growth in good shape (10)
27 Signs that might be clashing, people say (7)
28 Letter going on about very little (7)
29 It's not recorded as a rule (9,3)

DOWN

1 One doesn't snake silently around (7)
2 Grown soundlessly in the best sort of fungus (10)
3 Let tried organisation be given a new name (8)
4 Move with difficulty having some idea of getting clear (6)
5 Strong smell of brown dog-end (4)
6 Rock corrupt court with little work (7)
7 Islanders made angry by design (7,5)
10 Agreeing with Spain's mighty reforms (12)
13 In business to appear in television breaks (10)
15 Time to get right out of the cart (3)
18 Don't allow it when a person gives voice (8)
20 Not all soldiers provide a course of treatment (7)
22 Turn out not to be a warder (7)
23 Garment firm disturbing the rest (6)
26 Two couples are able to make it (4)

52

ACROSS

6 Give tongue to injuries after fighting (4,4,6)
9 One might be fired for having to slip out (6)
10 Spit up some Cheddar? (8)
11 Hate drug to become the issue (8)
13 Where income tax provides revenue (6)
15 Make wet physician relinquish leadership of magistrates (6)
17 Local area one found in sharp disorder (6)
19 Where to eat first when a small sibling comes round (6)
20 Condemnation in three articles by a person of learning (8)
22 Obvious chap to finish as a father (8)
24 Ability to become explosive about drink (6)
26 A drink from it may do you good (8,6)

DOWN

1 Salisbury presenting no problems? (5,3,6)
2 Northerner not heading for the races (4)
3 Having split the lot beg one to hold drink (6)
4 Ask was it possibly once an enemy sign (8)
5 Bit of luck needed to perform in a game (4)
7 Last to finish on the river (6)
8 Follow home the people to annoy because one denies others what one doesn't want (3,2,3,6)
12 Put energy into a blow for one to be entertained (5)
14 The French hit out at Scottish port (5)
16 Taking a cold break makes a man bad-tempered (8)
18 New build-up in the North-East (6)
21 Move to get first part of play performed (6)
23 Keen to help securing victory (4)
25 No longer with us after a time (4)

53

ACROSS

1 Sporting break when not fully employed (4-4)
5 Teachers giving a girl some spice (6)
9 Like Mary in opposition (8)
10 One's engaged in face of uncertainty (6)
12 Not quite happening to be on the level (4)
13 Not to be relied on to be at home without a break (10)
15 Check flower taking a new form (13)
19 Such fun is not to be expected (8,5)
23 Laid cities out with visionary effect (10)
25 Don't go when support is needed (4)
28 Capital as at the time included (6)
29 Shell something moving quickly (8)
30 Pulling to one side (6)
31 One swings fruit around the last turn (8)

DOWN

1 Game point missed by an artist (6)
2 Thrust with energy after a breather (5)
3 Ground for thinking there'll be racing here (4)
4 Very little time for one to hide in waving corn like a fool (7)
6 They might be counted as parts of the army (5)
7 Restore a place that might give one a wrong impression (9)
8 Hi when a Scot is feeling low? (8)
11 Not having much work coming up otherwise (4)
14 Foreign drink providing support at last (4)
15 Hear worse distortions of entertainment in a box (5-4)
16 Act just like an animal (3)
17 Killing many people leaving the land (4)
18 Hopeful to see a country captured in past revolution (8)
20 Special forces taking hotel in an encirclement (4)
21 Edge into protection of head churchman (7)
22 My clue to deconstruction in college (6)
24 Material way to reach the Pole (5)
26 Find a way to follow behind (5)
27 One may be waved in magical deception (4)

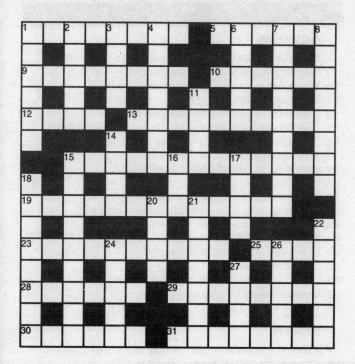

54

ACROSS

1 Move faster than deer to blame someone else (4,3,4)
9 Mistake not appreciated on your side (3,4)
10 Weave new net clumsily around one (7)
11 Listen, don't start getting in a flap (3)
12 Double rejection being involved therein (7)
13 Comfortable back where it's warm and there's firing (7)
14 One gets carried away by no royal performance in the street (3)
15 Mature writer having taken a bit of a risk (5)
17 He doesn't do much to give you a buzz (5)
18 Clever enough to be able to make cuts (5)
20 Prepare to make a submission at a lower level (5)
22 A rabble-rouser can make thumping good use of it (3)
24 Wicked devil acknowledging debts (7)
25 Hide away in a corner of an island (7)
26 Drink a little one (3)
27 Top African person given a deal of trouble (7)
28 Mean to declare time taken (7)
29 Talk a lot of giving Judy's co-star a blow (6-5)

DOWN

1 It should give point to one's writing (6-9)
2 Suppress the second one to have a baby (7)
3 He provides cover until Eric has him imprisoned (5)
4 Combine in finishing the sentence that's coming out (9)
5 Not able to issue proper notes (7)
6 One honoured to be involved in the clean-up? (6,2,3,4)
7 Consort with a superior person beside the cooker (6)
8 Courage needed to sound hard (6)
16 Asian offered IPA sank it uneasily (9)
18 Get the shakes in a dance (6)
19 Demonstrate that Burns initially offered a piece of folk wisdom (7)
21 Reading supporter (7)
23 One offers drink in a jug at both ends of the bar (6)
25 Give an impression of petulance (5)

55

ACROSS

1 Not everyone's idea of a soldier (7)
5 Cut what is nice out (6)
9 Think how exchanging one letter for an earlier one can give further time in office (2-5)
10 Unhappy after having trouble gaining unusual ends (7)
11 Blackjack? (3)
12 Once matured the great ferment inside can be overdone (11)
13 It's on the shoulders of a writer if libel starts (5)
14 Pleased if I'd get fair treatment (9)
16 Hanger-on coming to a quiet conclusion when an attendant is around (9)
17 Female member of the Champagne set (5)
19 Always friendly enough to accommodate poor Peter and you finally (11)
22 He would be able to cope, given time (3)
23 He thinks of himself as having got one into the wrong set (7)
24 Bring aid to man and woman by the river (7)
26 Free the betrayer captured by soldiers (6)
27 Lines about to be included in trials (7)

DOWN

1 Very good pay deals for those outside the law (7)
2 Room here for some very cool selling (3-5,7)
3 Time for only half the business of the meeting (3)
4 There's more to be won in the next race perhaps (5)
5 Make one get in another way at speed (9)
6 Supporter of no standing (5)
7 figures needed to give protection (6,2,7)
8 Did leg movement that allowed smooth progress to be made (6)
12 She's said to have two letters (5)
14 Enjoys success to some degree (9)
15 The thing lay around the country (5)
16 Worcester and Blenheim for instance (6)
18 They give voice in order to gain ingress maybe (7)
20 Be the second into the escape route (5)
21 Song of the year in Gaelic at last! (5)
25 Don't stand for deception (3)

56

ACROSS

1 Horse girl taking on the others to get the highest rise (5,7)

8 Funny to get one pound returned in salary improvement (7)

9 Encourage in hours of uncertainty (7)

11 Release Oriental friend concealing awful panic (10)

12 Entertain the idea that bad behaviour is good (4)

14 Songster running slap into trouble when visibility is bad (8)

16 Emotional problem making further talk impossible (4-2)

17 Had a session a day (3)

19 Excursion to expose what's been hidden (6)

21 Being German I get into a sticky situation when styles are mixed (8)

24 It's hard to remove wrinkles (4)

25 Old army officers run section badly (10)

27 Passage taken out of a pamphlet (7)

28 Opposed to becoming a census-taker? (7)

29 One needs a partner in seeking to make a contract (6,6)

DOWN

1 Cosmetic mother used to hide a mark (7)

2 Not getting to be inappropriate? (10)

3 Enter forbidden territory to do wrong (8)

4 It's in Navy manoeuvres you detect futility (6)

5 Right to be dismissed for defeat (4)

6 Leaving port of top quality in support (7)

7 It shows one's classical side (5,7)

10 Her pig rushes can be very persuasive (4-8)

13 Go on a horse to hide the Archbishop (10)

15 Knock a man up (3)

18 Diplomacy applied to one state for short-term advantage (8)

20 One runs to help support a pig (7)

22 Small farm credit giving Forte a problem (7)

23 Pay up and be comfortable (6)

26 Help an employee can give (4)

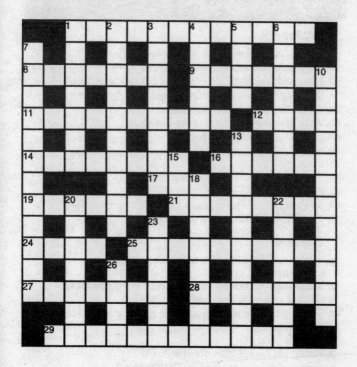

57

ACROSS

6 First effort to give a clue to identity? (7,7)

9 False turn, odd turn, finishing the dance (6)

10 Unkissed female possibly seen as belonging to the city (8)

11 One might be a chiseller in the matter of figures (8)

13 A very forceful man in a fight (6)

15 Anticipate a new arrival in the family (6)

17 Following a greeting in turn (6)

19 Weak Left extremists not present at a money-raising event (6)

20 Along with other things not specified (2,6)

22 Anything in the German issue (8)

24 Surprisingly offensive claim to represent growth (6)

26 Confidence of being own master (4-10)

DOWN

1 Where one's well known to have a topping experience (8,2,4)

2 Rank finally achieved by one of the Palace crowd (4)

3 Get Sid around to deal with food (6)

4 Where guidance is given as to the cheapest accommodation for voyagers (8)

5 Chapter-head (4)

7 Hiring out horses in uniform style (6)

8 Now and then transposed by Carlyle (4,3,7)

12 Drinks starting early in error (5)

14 Distracting movement if net is removed (5)

16 Achievement of all the world (8)

18 Loose pieces of cabbage finally devoured by wild birds (6)

21 Santa making first entry as part of the contract (6)

23 Talent for presentation (4)

25 Flying creature consuming one tempting item (4)

58

ACROSS

1 Heaving of bust in science fiction for sentimental effect (3-5)
5 She's returned the flowers and the drink (6)
9 Horse making last move to confront a fierce animal (8)
10 Be quiet when taking round prim little creature (6)
12 Go round and head off a bear (4)
13 Sent to be killed (10)
15 Hostile as well as amiable when offered a drink . . . (4,3,6)
19 . . . of unbelievable unpotability? (4,2,7)
23 Bribed to hide end badly wasted (10)
25 Said to have trouble reaching a higher level (4)
28 Fools do it wrong when one's around (6)
29 Reduce speed after a fashion (8)
30 Lets in another way to become part of the force (6)
31 Profitable use of money not in official clothing (8)

DOWN

1 Method of ordering my sets (6)
2 Get weaving in a second attack (5)
3 Prepare the ground for keeping the takings (4)
4 State of fair old tizzy (7)
6 Not affected by a strike (5)
7 Paddy's worry about what to provide for dinner (5,4)
8 Drink with a girl to get a line suitable for inscription (8)
11 Not having started to be recorded or copied (4)
14 Novel action – throwing a pound into the pool (4)
15 Rather erratic at telling the temperature? (9)
16 Refuse to give direction this time (3)
17 One newspaper dropping first-class input in lazy style (4)
18 It's raised in pursuit to inflict punishment (8)
20 Take off as the lady in question would (4)
21 A weekend taken this way seems to me magnificent (7)
22 A trail leading to higher achievement (6)
24 They may be taken as reminders that money is needed (5)
26 Stone the chief and French will rise (5)
27 Striking regularly (4)

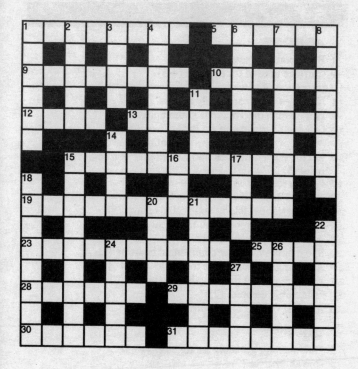

59

ACROSS

1 Be a sport – honestly! (4,3,4)
9 Carriage needed for eviction (4-3)
10 Indication of catch brought back into harbour (7)
11 No way a shop can supply mineral (3)
12 Fellow man in a religious community (7)
13 One isn't sure how to act the awkward brute (7)
14 Means of giving guidance without hot growth (3)
15 Let the dog come back and he will give you something frilly (5)
17 Girl on the platform with you at first (5)
18 Fated to drop the wrong set as one ate (5)
20 The snag about taking your pet to church (5)
22 He's left the shrubbery to find transport (3)
24 Animal city, New York (7)
25 Shout approval about commercial boasting (7)
26 Annoying not being able to sing at a meal (3)
27 We stare around for something to put on (7)
28 Game little creature (7)
29 Another view of the prophet's gift (6-5)

DOWN

1 They haven't got a big act together (10,5)
2 One alternative (7)
3 One can teach a workers' group to take on the Right (5)
4 Convenient device that might be profitable (9)
5 A reason for thinking a navigational error has been made (7)
6 Current means of keeping warm after retirement (8,7)
7 As safe as horses? (6)
8 Strong leadership for a regiment in review (6)
16 Corny mystery about a fool in atomic research apparatus (9)
18 Lower people with qualifications in a flow (6)
19 Rids act of extreme complication (7)
21 Faculty inquiry (7)
23 Even without outstanding features (6)
25 Supports some of the players (5)

60

ACROSS

1 Regarding a supporter as so backward (7)
5 It's obvious the old man needs shelter (6)
9 Canny little girl making an impression (7)
10 Disinclination to move one and retain circulation (7)
11 Put one's foot down without starting punishment (3)
12 Counties not disposed to be in disagreement (11)
13 Put off being respectful (5)
14 Not paying to be kept above the waterline (9)
16 Have again to take back (9)
17 Craft chat having to be translated at the end of the day (5)
19 William's heart makes him a help to advertisers (11)
22 Fit quietly away to have a sporting time (3)
23 Exciting enough to get people out of bed (7)
24 Turn in awful rotter for cruel treatment (7)
26 Attempt to follow the intelligence of superior people (6)
27 Rustic fodder issue (7)

DOWN

1 Wished to find a snake – with possibly dire result (7)
2 Drinks provided to show appreciation? (5,2,8)
3 Something to eat for one in the gym (3)
4 Appeal to beat the devil (5)
5 Lice wriggling in papers – very funny! (9)
6 River water in fast flow, not otherwise (5)
7 County cover (8,7)
8 Went beyond examination success (6)
12 Characters in suits? (5)
14 With touches of emotion (9)
15 One pays to be put in possession (5)
16 Dress that's right for a man (6)
18 Do badly with nurse around at last (4-3)
20 Hold back when there's a day's work to do (5)
21 Get royalty when you produce a design for a ship (5)
25 Make light of having to reveal the wager's lost (3)

61

ACROSS

1 Someone enchanting of the creepy kind (5-7)
8 Tells when there is a connection (7)
9 Here before being dispatched (7)
11 It lets one see what scope there is for an exposure (10)
12 Strike a priest (4)
14 They can secure a person with twisted laces (8)
16 An expert ascribes it to the currency's zero loss (6)
17 Accurately reproduced from classical epic poetry (3)
19 Message for one in awful slang (6)
21 Set attendants on an animal that goes wild (8)
24 Being foreign he's gone back to the bar girl (4)
25 Shake curl in cool move to be seen as a local worthy (10)
27 Make profitable use of an accomplishment (7)
28 Robber group with hidden equipment (7)
29 Influential person showing the way ahead (7,5)

DOWN

1 Lives wild with sailors of rich appearance (7)
2 Fair italic letters made to look contrived (10)
3 Members of an ancient sect covering Caesar's head in oils (8)
4 One conveys something by jumping (6)
5 Bird man in the academy (4)
6 Mad reel around the green (7)
7 Something seriously wrong at interment (5,7)
10 Destroy evidence of sorrow that's rubbish to Marxists (4,2,6)
13 Extraordinary girl's turnover on the way up (10)
15 You the teacher, man? (3)
18 One finds people of consuming interest (8)
20 Get to grips with the top of green fruit (7)
22 Not afraid to be attentive to ladies (7)
23 Security attachment in town (6)
26 Valid for all time (4)

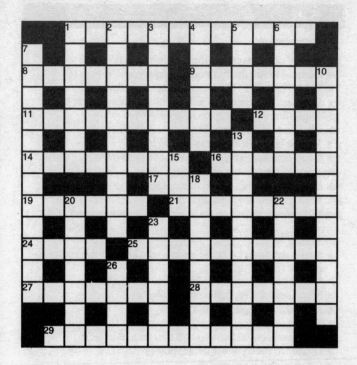

62

ACROSS

6 Friday's employer sets the bird boy on a new course (8,6)

9 Coming to see there's a commercial opening here (6)

10 Tubby hugs the old boxing champion to death (8)

11 Be respectful about the aim of one meeting an attack (8)

13 Slight further application of polish (6)

15 Character in a temper (6)

17 Stay to keep the master in check (6)

19 Good man sore afflicted by lots of things (6)

20 Not still finding the others inferior (8)

22 Spiritual adviser in need of tea, that's obvious (8)

24 Force person to give a little money (6)

26 Time to say what you think could be a turning point (8,6)

DOWN

1 Carl's the dancer – could be one who pursues a very young partner (6-8)

2 Clever message getting the head to go off (4)

3 Made one of a football team maybe (6)

4 No clansmen here without penalty (4-4)

5 Influence not exercised by a backer? (4)

7 Where one could learn to make an animal cross (6)

8 Unable to touch down for support (3,2,4,5)

12 Go in to make a record (5)

14 Cry out about royal battle (5)

16 Have another look for something studious to do (8)

18 Engineer having to move and be left outside (6)

21 Little time to find the right part (6)

23 The way to get a stroke when it's hot (4)

25 One may go to sea from a holiday resort (4)

63

ACROSS

1 Waves of paint (8)
5 He's learned the day the carrier gets in (6)
9 Furnished with a condition (8)
10 Force business representative on the Spanish (6)
12 Spoils sound instrument (4)
13 One looks for a way to sort copper out (10)
15 One's relatively unsophisticated out of town (7,6)
19 The miser next door? (4,9)
23 Missile launcher activated with a blow (10)
25 She appears in school games as a star player (4)
28 Sound conductor (6)
29 Think one might go round one gallery (8)
30 Force to take a turn in what one's wearing (6)
31 Nasty due to being erratic (8)

DOWN

1 Provide in a flexible way (6)
2 A fight in the neighbourhood (5)
3 One of those that might provide a fishy accompaniment (4)
4 Performer of rubbish at a seaside establishment (7)
6 A sailor leaves the shellfish for the sole (5)
7 Stew of tripe and peas to get a meal going (9)
8 Learn to be adaptable in what you drink without prejudice (8)
11 Catch sight of an English agent (4)
14 Flow of hot water? (4)
15 Get hot and react differently according to temperament (9)
16 Tease into fury, almost (3)
17 Music-maker's order to conceal nothing (4)
18 Brilliant spin round getting one flushed (8)
20 Put pressure on to get lines removed (4)
21 Worked on a farm and won outing for a dance (7)
22 Linen neckline (6)
24 Sportsmen drive towards them keeping on course (5)
26 A fix set up for a climber (5)
27 It could put one on a higher level (4)

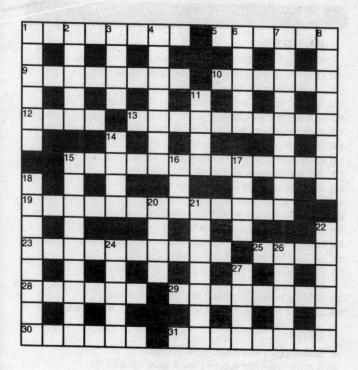

64

ACROSS

1 Not much grit as if on tour in superior surroundings (5,2,4)
9 Draw near round the dump for a get-together (7)
10 Given too much to be dealt with internally (7)
11 Animal to follow (3)
12 Joy at Stacey's dancing (7)
13 Where Gene gets together with Tim (7)
14 Ready to make a collection (3)
15 Look sullen when put down (5)
17 All those people in an Oxford college (5)
18 Nothing else can hold one that swings (5)
20 Don't start trouble if it's not one thing (5)
22 Strike as being a touch backward (3)
24 Search and find enough drink for a thousand years (7)
25 Malicious creature joining actress when one holds a ball (7)
26 Refusal to make any amendment (3)
27 Being judged to have lost energy as an unhappy relation (2,5)
28 Shut up person in prison and impose a penalty (7)
29 There'll be an explosion when one's given the chuck (4-7)

DOWN

1 End of court proceedings (4,3,3,5)
2 A great Cockney greeting for a lady's maid (7)
3 Not having enough point when eyed askance (5)
4 Forcibly remove creature of dubious charm (4-5)
5 Having nothing to show for years of lurching on sea-legs (7)
6 It's hard to know what's best to take (9,6)
7 Something you gain when you go in (6)
8 Sayings of the year go on a long time (6)
16 False supporter (6,3)
18 Cause great distress at school (6)
19 Delight in making one of the family a non-starter (7)
21 Building plan in circulation (7)
23 He should be able to carry his drink (6)
25 Get moving and do a round (5)

65

ACROSS

1 Nightmare in a Caribbean state endlessly confronting America (7)
5 Moves aimlessly in the snow (6)
9 Sinful as anything in New York (7)
10 The day Reg got restless and left, the dog! (7)
11 The central reality that reveals depression (3)
12 Being weak can be fine if perhaps one's in the money (11)
13 Waste the final hour in sleep (5)
14 Extra numbers needed to cover a man's supporters (4-5)
16 Discussed what might be awarded (9)
17 Not an idle loafer (5)
19 Question in the gallery when Roger wanders in (11)
22 He'll get a beating if he appears again! (3)
23 Disable many with a slight wave (7)
24 Dispose of more in an open-air location (7)
26 Time Nancy turned out an article for the organisation (6)
27 Believers in God having set this out (7)

DOWN

1 Eroding badly if not attended to (7)
2 Freely awarded foreign title will have no significance (5,3,7)
3 Disgust expressed at the custom of turning up without it (3)
4 Rage at receiving some nasty letters (5)
5 Those unable to speak start to cause astonishment (9)
6 Ten less than pleasant columns of Greek (5)
7 A number of gunmen have achieved novel fame (5,10)
8 Pastel varied in pictures for a book (6)
12 Send out for a paper (5)
14 Just covering a bribe set up with intent (9)
15 Fellow with the capacity to give you the story (5)
16 Settle for an embrace (6)
18 Rabbits on hikes (7)
20 Get ready to satisfy the consumer (5)
21 Up there where storage space might be available (5)
25 One of the possible objectives when one goes on a bender (3)

66

ACROSS

1 Shy when serving teas one's taken before the event (8,4)
8 Doesn't favour work attitudes (7)
9 Rang lad to come round and deliver flowers (7)
11 Senior officer with time for robbery (10)
12 Warning that means nothing to some people (4)
14 Instruction to finish sport when it's wet (8)
16 Account for having to make a 50 per cent reduction (6)
17 Fat man dropping by for some ice-cream maybe (3)
19 Royal stand-in (6)
21 Almost fail to see a game that doesn't tally (8)
24 They may be pulled back to get one going (4)
25 Playful coils tangled in a Somerset town (10)
27 Irish airport has trouble when new start gets turned down in Paris (7)
28 Glad to see you might be having a word on the mat (7)
29 One dim maiden develops into a shady lady (4-8)

DOWN

1 Something very like chopped plaice – right on! (7)
2 Carrying American marking outside (10)
3 Someone local making payment to accommodate the players (8)
4 Hire to get involved (6)
5 Bring about order of a kind (4)
6 I intend to rise in a motoring body but energy is lacking (7)
7 Sport coat mob in fighting formation (6,6)
10 Removal men may gather here (3,2,7)
13 Rats almost given confinement before one provides food (10)
15 Face up to a sticky experience (3)
18 Flowed in waves when an account was due to be paid (8)
20 Relevant to Ms Greer's one deficiency (7)
22 Pull up in a temper showing more than one colour (3-4)
23 Quick to declare the expert not out (6)
26 Not in favour of finishing the Italian wine (4)

67

ACROSS

6 Notable person with something to say? (6,2,6)
9 Force to move support with a novelist's heart (6)
10 Fuss at a difficult point in taking on responsibility (8)
11 Supposing there's a take-over (8)
13 A large glass of spirit to put me right (6)
15 Approach with the bill that shows what has to be paid (6)
17 What a handsome chap a fellow is! (6)
19 Inclined to shut one's eyes and give dodgy character shelter inside (6)
20 Have Paul thrown out when there's disorder (8)
22 Taking great pride in being a royal bird (8)
24 Line round the Eastern Mediterranean given short treatment (6)
26 Not much that's worth a lot (8,6)

DOWN

1 People are entertained by his sharp intake (5-9)
2 A little bit of a decline (4)
3 Hot stuff might seem cold to one (6)
4 Protected from the destruction of our dream (8)
5 Occasion to get up and give out (4)
7 Tree seen around on the mountains (6)
8 State of America with its Communist layer (5,6,3)
12 Relative taking the pledge (5)
14 It's crazy for a country not to back gold (5)
16 High-flying clergyman (3-5)
18 Growth of Good American pursuit of enjoyment (6)
21 As an author Rider Haggard concealed what might be unpleasant (6)
23 The impudence to embrace with affection! (4)
25 That's the final check friend! (4)

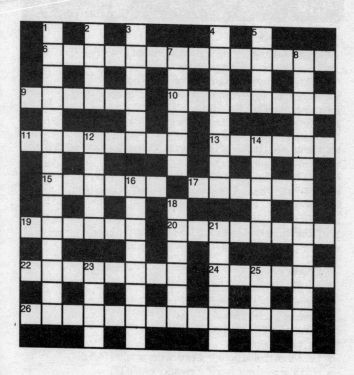

68

ACROSS

1 Dark look suggesting one is the victim of a strike (5,3)
5 Drink to cause a stoppage (6)
9 Scary navigation exercise to get into port (8)
10 Very great comedian second to make an entrance (6)
12 Connection left fluid (4)
13 One gets a thousand extra for capturing heroic William by a bloomer (10)
15 Get bogged down as one who lacks imagination (5-2-3-3)
19 Achieve a smooth equality (4,6,3)
23 Not the sort to head for cruelty (10)
25 One might leave flying to travel in an old ship (4)
28 Form a new association in fact (6)
29 Exit to one side if unqualified (8)
30 Using the towel end round the back of the ear (6)
31 One protects the last to get freed to move around (8)

DOWN

1 Carrier let out to cause a stir (6)
2 Stage of domestic work? (5)
3 Give up excitement (4)
4 Concealment for all but Eastern eyes (7)
6 Strike influence (5)
7 Let Mimi dance before it closes the session (4,5)
8 Had a nice excursion in a country estate (8)
11 What a blessing no former pupil turned up! (4)
14 Have an inclination to register (4)
15 Talk as if it's simple to find a place to drink (5-4)
16 Having fish around would make the house seem foreign (3)
17 Where one might get one's eye in after a ferry ride (4)
18 Needed some paper when in debt (8)
20 Island of international importance (4)
21 Wave the guest off and be about to follow (7)
22 Give treatment when caught in an opening (6)
24 Material gathered from many long researches (5)
26 That's the right idea – remove heat elements without bending (5)
27 Lake restaurant losing money (4)

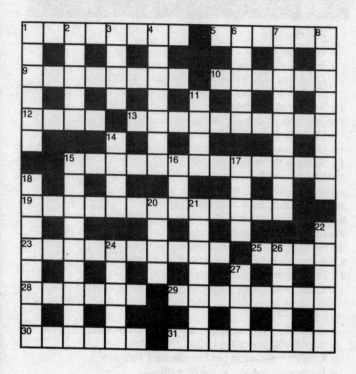

69

ACROSS

1 As a partner one's bound to display it (7-4)
9 Yearning for Peter to show some style (7)
10 Get round to pen love letters in a new way (7)
11 Don't work without a pound being earned (3)
12 Regard as a senior policeman (7)
13 Numbers of missing miners drive an RAF man wild (7)
14 Hill men leave the guide (3)
15 One is among creatures returning looking brown (5)
17 Spirit of the new and big (5)
18 She's inside being made less gauche and shy (5)
20 One's in the saddle, it may be added (5)
22 Fix to come back for a drink (3)
24 The way to get water transport going (7)
25 Sally may be getting top rise (7)
26 Time of uncertain obliteration (3)
27 Racecourse figure in shirt with jazzy stripe (7)
28 Display ten in the course of play (7)
29 Look round to see if there might be iron on Crete (11)

DOWN

1 It enables progress to be made with a clear outlook (10,5)
2 Superior figure of the French game (7)
3 Clumsy write-up in the International Times (5)
4 Berry aged to look an old man (9)
5 Transposed for poetic use (7)
6 It ensures one's going to be richly rewarded (6,9)
7 Be quick to present a second picture (6)
8 They come from the centre to join the outer circle (6)
16 Tailless fish followed by bird and horse (9)
18 Use tat ingeniously to look smart (6)
19 Able to expand marketing rise with sudden movement (7)
21 Hit on drink as an expression of sympathy (7)
23 About to give direction in standard anticipation of fighting (3-3)
25 Means of telling one's in the wrong road (5)

70

ACROSS

1 Leave the ranks of those who agree (4,3)
5 Give orders to go straight (6)
9 Backward boys able to go in for gossip (7)
10 Make a fuss about the health centre being sort of triangular (7)
11 Work written in American English (3)
12 Parson at inn prepared to be open-minded (3-8)
13 Gain admission to the record book (5)
14 Sort of talc that sets the TV serial's mood (9)
16 Put on trial for writing that has some appeal (9)
17 There's little credit in giving help for burning (5)
19 What's left of it can change in this place outside (11)
22 A couple of pounds and that's the lot! (3)
23 Tell how to cook fine cod (7)
24 Command a girl to accommodate the wrong set (7)
26 Go into it for a break (6)
27 Signified not being in action (7)

DOWN

1 Social security payment certain to cause a split (7)
2 Don't be sure who will benefit from your will (5,2,2,6)
3 Strange ring for a theologian (3)
4 It's sharp to conclude investment with a loan conversion (5)
5 Paris rebuilt in time to look quite different (9)
6 Something to eat when rubbish is brought round (5)
7 A number of people trying to find mates (5,10)
8 Can see the difference made by a spirited gathering (6)
12 Bottle appearing when we have dinner very shortly (5)
14 They aren't entitled to be in residence (9)
15 Level of achievement in an actor's career (5)
16 Royal publicity management in church (6)
18 Late action taken about song (7)
20 It's water under the bridge at Cologne (5)
21 Turn on crazy wanderer (5)
25 Harbour no degree of evil (3)

71

ACROSS

1 Scale of money conversion effecting no real saving (5,7)
8 Standing for being honest (7)
9 One calls for the thing to be covered by feature protection (7)
11 Habitual attire even when on the move (10)
12 Not so much teaching on departure (4)
14 When a pal's around you won't find him starting bitterness (8)
16 Hey, that's magically quick! (6)
17 The previous sparkle that gets a girl back (3)
19 Composed of some seed and fruit (6)
21 Less satisfactory surroundings for a right-hand charger (3-5)
24 Expel from the most prestigious top position (4)
25 Originator of awful riot after receiving expert information (10)
27 Offered backing about noise avoiding (7)
28 Inspire an Ulster friend (7)
29 It's said a girl putting on weight gets chaps to start talking (12)

DOWN

1 Always otherwise during illness (7)
2 Authorised to run with one pal (10)
3 Starting ten turns on the eastern circuit (8)
4 A victory in place of depression (6)
5 The closest are leaving home (4)
6 Test arm movement that has some importance (7)
7 Notes on paper for twenty players? (7,5)
10 Make a calm comeback as policemen might (7,5)
13 Able to grasp how her pen perhaps produces devious lies (10)
15 Second person said to be able to name a tree (3)
18 Damage the resting-place of a noble foreigner (8)
20 Scorn what might be said during a row (7)
22 Withdraw what's said about a pamphlet (7)
23 Get round the outfit in the beginning (6)
26 Where missiles are held back from targeting the metropolis (4)

72

ACROSS

6 They're up to expressing surprise over vision (6,8)
9 Not the sort to be cruel (6)
10 He wants to dispose of the mess Alan made (8)
11 Pay out for having finally received awful bruises (8)
13 Point that should amount to nothing (6)
15 Soldiers of the line? (6)
17 Right support to provide at either end (6)
19 Credit is doubled when there's an emergency (6)
20 Disobliging on the other hand (8)
22 Not quite a simple pursuit of advantage (8)
24 Declining to ring work when it's not raining outside (6)
26 Leading painter superior to force (5,9)

DOWN

1 Imbiber's depression facilitating beastly absorption (8,6)
2 Miss Miller's beginnings as an opera girl (4)
3 Mulled ale raising the colour of the one in front (6)
4 City man being the last member to take ship (8)
5 Lady showing the flag (4)
7 Time for a consumer to get round to start shopping (6)
8 Waving wheat might be the proper indicator of conditions to come (7,7)
12 Boldness needed to make money (5)
14 Superior meal not having a soup starter (5)
16 I would rise and take a position some way off (8)
18 Don't let people see what film is on (6)
21 Cover missing when you hear fresh song (6)
23 Sailors who sounded boastful (4)
25 Eyes looking round (4)

73

ACROSS

1 Chief medical officer in Sherwood maybe (8)
5 Understanding cover (6)
9 Forces a woman to take in one merry with drink (8)
10 It enables you to get at the tinned food for a start (6)
12 Some of what our Dutch friends say in a foreign language (4)
13 Superior source of the higher learning (5-5)
15 Sage advice for Mods' widows maybe (5,2,6)
19 Faith so firm it's almost incredible (4,2,7)
23 Divorced partner greeting the part one put on show (10)
25 Bill being the man to feel yearning (4)
28 Models a new look for ladies (6)
29 Heaven is being in the show (8)
30 Be quick to get out of Athens (6)
31 Mend a dud somehow by putting something on (8)

DOWN

1 Well known to be the fellow who cut a timid creature's tail off (6)
2 Made straight use of power (5)
3 Little one said to have great power (4)
4 Lines of military authority (7)
6 Like a small illustration of jelly (5)
7 Beg to get a grip on a vessel (9)
8 Boring occasion Rose is involved in (8)
11 One was bound to work on the land (4)
14 Documentary exercise of law and order (4)
15 Overpriced if the value is zero (9)
16 Poetry due to be spoken (3)
17 Very cool shake of the dice (4)
18 Embarrassed to be seen as one of the flock (8)
20 Send the choppers into action (4)
21 Animal standard in dole distribution (7)
22 Have another think and win back (6)
24 I'm leaving Belgium when expansion is possible (5)
26 It's grand when your daughter has one! (5)
27 A piece of this should present no difficulty (4)

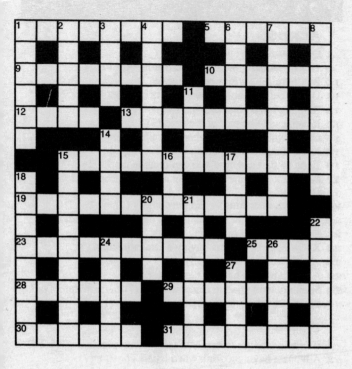

74

ACROSS

1 Quite sure to be late (4,7)
9 Too threadbare for personal cover indoors (7)
10 Bet there'll be wings on the move (7)
11 Don't feel well able to take time off at last (3)
12 Ribs broken a great deal back in port (7)
13 It happens to be part of the soap (7)
14 One might get a break when new life emerges (3)
15 Make it a rule to put on a play (5)
17 Time to start seeing if you can remove marks (5)
18 Drink about a quarter of a pint and move from side to side (5)
20 Sport rally not finishing in the country (5)
22 Failure to connect with acid head detained by doctor (3)
24 Keep up with us in making a mark (7)
25 Knowledge of flowers having a fatal attraction (7)
26 A girl from Madagascar (3)
27 Awful labs may have to be rebuilt (7)
28 Spinners look good in rumpled dress (7)
29 Sin with a single lousy tumble by mistake (11)

DOWN

1 Be smart enough to notch up fashion achievements (2,6,2,5)
2 Advocate having a drink when letters come in (7)
3 Is a learner able to make a cut? (5)
4 One may think one is able to make a light return (9)
5 Insulting American quartet in Lincoln (7)
6 Where country pictures can be seen in London (8,7)
7 Put together with stone (6)
8 Temple band said to lack warmth (6)
16 Response to stress when Anne gets involved with the Laird (9)
18 Smooth move to provide special troops with fodder (6)
19 Take measure to spoil proper use of language (7)
21 Means of conveying some of the risks in changing roles (7)
23 Service conductor (6)
25 Give a girl a ring to effect a tie-up (5)

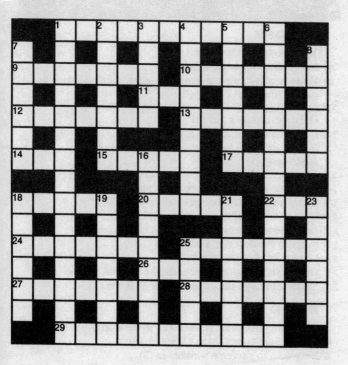

75

ACROSS

1 Met dire trouble for a fault (7)
5 Last of the kids to have fame (6)
9 Right to allow free movement between opening prison and our leaving court (7)
10 Something funny about a girl being very strict (7)
11 Have the law on a girl (3)
12 Her moves are attractive in a middling way (5-6)
13 It does you good to get pleasantly free from city attachment (5)
14 Cordially welcoming when it's plain one has a gun (4-5)
16 Fine time to say something about retirement (4,5)
17 In distributing dole one gets rather tipsy (5)
19 Object to flexibility teasing the brain (4-7)
22 Englishman in Australia returning to clean up (3)
23 Sings in the shirt one's put on (7)
24 Loan needed to get ahead (7)
26 One might cut out what sounds like wisdom otherwise (6)
27 Seeping through the big growth around one (7)

DOWN

1 Something put down is turned up in the warehouse (7)
2 Wrong time to rate inane Queen (5,10)
3 Very easy to smuggle whiskey in (3)
4 Rum and some beer – that's the lot! (5)
5 Trap enemy into giving money back (9)
6 She's not quite the one to make a conquest (5)
7 Nothing to pay when courtesy is shown (4,11)
8 Used to being ruined when thrown out (6)
12 Success brought home by a philosopher (5)
14 One arranges for a bag to have interior divisions (9)
15 Where you get when you keep moving (5)
16 Move like a doctor in one's manner of walking (6)
18 Cause misery by notes and papers (7)
20 Extra smell at sunrise (5)
21 State aid distributed by the Home Office (5)
25 Energy of six thousand Romans (3)

76

ACROSS

1 Committee investigating Labour? (7,5)
8 Fired for making a hash of dieting (7)
9 Use central force when it's difficult to see where fruit can be obtained (7)
11 Bind an apprentice in the works as a means of getting going (10)
12 Knock out a crazy return (4)
14 Using building skill to get nicer arrangement (8)
16 Line of bricks to show the way (6)
17 Object to returning in an old boat (3)
19 Devotion to somewhere hot in North America (6)
21 What gets a wheel turning in a works contest (8)
24 Get a line for an urgent message (4)
25 Mind being powerful and stubborn (10)
27 Dissipated character absorbing money in the usual way (7)
28 Account of reform without trickery (7)
29 Bear smelling out museum treasures (5,7)

DOWN

1 Gain a few by being charming (7)
2 Going back to see a sailor about tree chopping (10)
3 One don somehow gets advanced without doing much (8)
4 Reason for having been through the mill (6)
5 Chief appearance in a familiar church structure (4)
6 One betrays rising skill organising a riot (7)
7 Easy solution to a herbal problem (6,6)
10 Means of getting work done by an ass? (6-6)
13 Security provided by another branch of the family (10)
15 Northerners swear by it in a sticky situation (3)
18 Difficult situation finished subject to legal obligation (4,4)
20 Devious rival capturing the workers' organisation in all but name (7)
22 Nothing easing awful pains (7)
23 Get back and have another think (6)
26 King William's fruity origins (4)

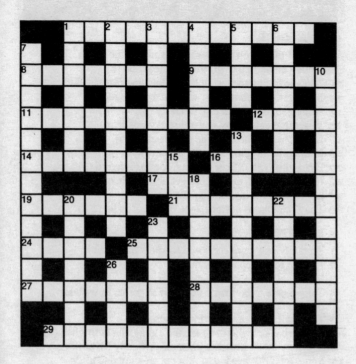

77

ACROSS

6 Does it make you wonder if the stuff is edible? (4,3,7)
9 Obtain an animal to go back for sea food (6)
10 Always failing to start opening the wine (8)
11 Not taking much interest without a catalogue (8)
13 Not celebrated for heroic modesty (6)
15 Vegetable offered by general sticky inside (6)
17 Little beast embracing the female child (6)
19 Man with the skills to make a suit (6)
20 Final turn with officer one regarded as a friend (8)
22 One has to push and pull to get notes from one (8)
24 Reprimand for invading space (6)
26 They're close to performance on TV or radio (6,8)

DOWN

1 Privately one's not supposed to know this (8,6)
2 Pay out to go separate ways (4)
3 Weak notes on a charity event (6)
4 Taking care to be firm when Horace comes in without one (8)
5 Take half a month to perform sport (4)
7 Make changes when you see the clergyman is English (6)
8 In a stew that's heated with some difficulty (3,3,8)
12 Some integrity needed to turn out an animal (5)
14 Play in a way that's odd (5)
16 An old animal person stood around inside (8)
18 Office furniture item (6)
21 Very hot dirt or mess (6)
23 Contemporary abandonment of navy fashion (4)
25 Punishment for producing sugar (4)

78

ACROSS

1 Yes, a quid could get you a tie-up here (8)
5 Test the woman who has children (6)
9 Find an animal before taking a run (8)
10 Jack and Jock meeting on the road maybe (6)
12 Take-away man (4)
13 One sees the future novelist taking one back inside (10)
15 It's uncultivated to have nothing on (5,2,6)
19 Present to stop the fighting (5,8)
23 One's too miserly to pay much for fish (10)
25 Mark of a second-rate bunch (4)
28 Record spread causing a hold-up (3-3)
29 One's take-off can be entertaining (8)
30 Make obscure study about old craft (6)
31 Quite an achievement of the girll's to get down (8)

DOWN

1 Pole taking one in for rum (6)
2 Tact being exercised about one in poor accommodation (5)
3 A girl starts to have time for an old sailor (4)
4 Don't like to have a Red Pole around (7)
6 An actor to ring up in Nebraska (5)
7 Powerless to get the sandwich filling tied up (9)
8 Instrument of justice (8)
11 One of those coming down in the fall (4)
14 Funeral party left behind when the ship sails (4)
15 Science used by one punishing the person who takes what's left (9)
16 One's a fool to hang around without a pound (3)
17 Bill has the instincts to be sharp (4)
18 Drag around two gallons in spots (8)
20 Part of the proof a Kennel Club pedigree isn't genuine (4)
21 Allow to give a name (7)
22 Legendary baby birds (6)
24 One has to leave the fish somewhere (5)
26 Run out in error (5)
27 Intake from foreign parliament (4)

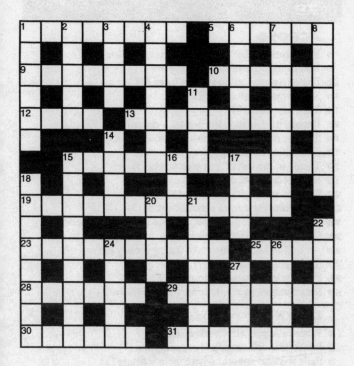

79

ACROSS

1 Incomprehensible couple there's no treating? (6,5)
9 Makes firm use of her sand (7)
10 Use of a racket to make a delivery (7)
11 Spinner at a high level (3)
12 They also serve (7)
13 Record it to include the person's description (7)
14 Strange copper and American leaving port (3)
15 Gets rid of some bags (5)
17 Throw in the last of a savage world (5)
18 Egg producer on the level (5)
20 Flow of work without effort (5)
22 Fancy making a loud announcement (3)
24 Bill comes back turning in and out when care is needed (7)
25 Girl clinging to a pole back in the wreckage (7)
26 As well as being a means of losing money (3)
27 Run and get some coal (7)
28 Wet treeless course in a circle (7)
29 Music-maker in revolutionary action (6-5)

DOWN

1 Where sleepers are on edge? (9,6)
2 Ineffective call to reduce consumption (7)
3 Fails to stand straight where there's tilting (5)
4 Spied Reds manoeuvring in various places (9)
5 Making a move where another way can be found (7)
6 Tall hat may be representing rage? (6,2,7)
7 Tall for a demonstrator (6)
8 Pay for a seat (6)
16 Tell niece to go out and get some customers (9)
18 Tree insect (6)
19 Revel in getting one into the list (7)
21 Give voice about getting the business right and achieving goals (7)
23 Injury time after a hold-up (6)
25 Sacrifice in order to escape (5)

80

ACROSS

1 Make tin legs sparkle (7)
5 Capacity for explosive drink intake (6)
9 Love to see a capital fellow on the juice at last! (7)
10 Build up people when talks start after a month (7)
11 Let people know the couple have lost a little money (3)
12 What you can see with glasses is impressive (11)
13 Shoot a junior member of the family (5)
14 Crush under a vessel brewing tea (9)
16 Taste Ireland on English fruit (9)
17 Trick to avoid a strike (5)
19 Possibly reprocessed by the one who was here earlier (11)
22 Carrier not encountered in a way (3)
23 Permitted cute capers enjoyed in our salad days (7)
24 Not paid by a friend to gain ulterior ends (7)
26 Old Roman transport getting round depression (6)
27 Enraged at being taken mistakenly for someone (7)

DOWN

1 People in Europe beginning to make a brief reply (7)
2 It raises the temperature when one gets stuck in (9,6)
3 Negative rise in weight (3)
4 She represents the sibling issue (5)
5 Easily persuaded to pull the wagon up on board (9)
6 It makes sense to record who's in charge (5)
7 One has an eye for the other in sewer employment (6,3,6)
8 Fall short of what's required as a consumer (6)
12 Produce a note with searing effect (5)
14 Don't turn so much round the one end that's weak (9)
15 Don't start laughing when you wash down below (5)
16 Couple of coins thrown into the hat for drink (6)
18 Approve Don's move in unusual language (7)
20 Break out in a natural rising at the report's conclusion (5)
21 Common talk of a dissolute woman around the Nag's Head (5)
25 She's made an appointment to take one of the Lawrences away (3)

81

ACROSS

1 Band judge able to keep track of a hearing (4-8)
8 Where high-fliers have a down-to-earth experience (7)
9 Brief periodical priest to return the mixture (7)
11 Physical strength might be applied to ref when Robert's around (5,5)
12 Article about to appear soon (4)
14 See grand use for missiles (8)
16 One fellow follows a large number in the mountains (6)
17 Make a knight provide a new sound-track (3)
19 Architectural leader in position to provide a great building (6)
21 Cake with rum in – gee, that's different (8)
24 Achieved comeback with a classical cover (4)
25 Something to do with sanction about shattered Ming (10)
27 Emergency means of contact during a blazing row (3,4)
28 Invent new way to find the right person to offer drink (7)
29 Had Red nicely baffled by a motor part (8-4)

DOWN

1 Moved quickly to cover routine rise in cruelty (7)
2 Source of article to be found in a part of France (10)
3 Artist having to dine out when food supply is limited (8)
4 Opportunity to take a risk (6)
5 Head away from Norfolk water this way (4)
6 Machines seen to be mixing drink inside (7)
7 Person with no ambition to repair growth area (7,5)
10 Literary figure able to invent characters (3,2,7)
13 Man going around caning wrong to show spite (10)
15 Endlessly compelled to set up calculation (3)
18 One accepts religiously what one's told (8)
20 Girl around the guest-house starting to try not very hard (7)
22 Gathered in accordance with the angle an editor requires (7)
23 Use a little science at last to get a rise (6)
26 She's been given two fine openings (4)

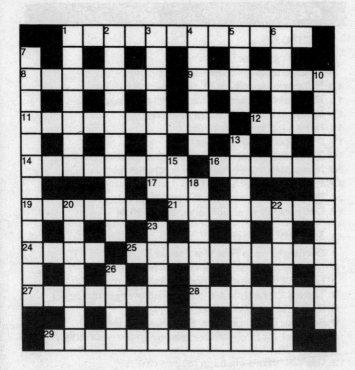

82

ACROSS

6 Taking off by car? (7,7)
9 Mean to open tin at last (6)
10 Not given tea perhaps (8)
11 Hop around backing topless wife's challenge (8)
13 Compete with girl's return in the city (6)
15 Lift a hand to a superior (6)
17 Bless you for that outburst! (6)
19 It's harder to spot a tree beside a foreign sea (6)
20 Name one fit to go back in to contradict (8)
22 Punishing sort of kiss (8)
24 Frank and the detectives coming round (6)
26 One goes dry as an unlikely relation (10,4)

DOWN

1 One might get to France at a stroke (7,7)
2 Discomfort suffered by a visitor – no way! (4)
3 Land Press chief with reports of rising all round (6)
4 Treated tolerantly when getting loud over gin maybe (8)
5 Help to be included where it's at (4)
7 Someone over there being the victim of a jerk (6)
8 Fine cure for Eve when harassed by government money man (7,7)
12 One can make a big hit in religion (5)
14 Standing up before getting caught short (5)
16 Rile Bert badly with awful effect (8)
18 One not in a union (6)
21 Make allowances for shift (6)
23 Bay for a bloke (4)
25 Old boatman refusing to become a leading harbour character (4)

83

ACROSS

1 Generous with looks (8)
5 Not happy at first being cruel (6)
9 A little bit of quiet writing (8)
10 It gets you through without going over the top (6)
12 Flat for a woman to own at last (4)
13 Coming to a river it's right that one should take chances (10)
15 One who thinks ritual important in a big religious build-up? (4,9)
19 They may not agree but there's something between them (8,5)
23 Choose to peck carelessly at a take-away (10)
25 Stimulate most of the football team (4)
28 Cause extremes of emotion at last (6)
29 Operatic ship's cover (8)
30 Plan to edge into part of the scenery (6)
31 Branch of Free State getting a laugh (8)

DOWN

1 Chap pensively wondering what might occur inside (6)
2 Bottle? No fear! (5)
3 Foreign beer served up by mistake (4)
4 Having a tune to set old mice dancing (7)
6 Announcement last month of one being in the majority (5)
7 One doesn't know how to spend a morning in rousing disorder (9)
8 Learn to relax in drink provided by the kind-hearted (8)
11 Lover of fashionable dress (4)
14 Contrives to get a man going for a long time (4)
15 Something in the beer and whisky game (9)
16 Good start away from the great shade (3)
17 Rules might be difficult to understand (4)
18 Shorten the business before getting into writings (8)
20 Gather there's something to eat (4)
21 The lady with the jazz accompaniment, a star performer (7)
22 One isn't free to go under it (6)
24 Producer of colours holding teacher up in the afternoon (5)
26 Picture the post office with its warm interior (5)
27 Singer in the swim (4)

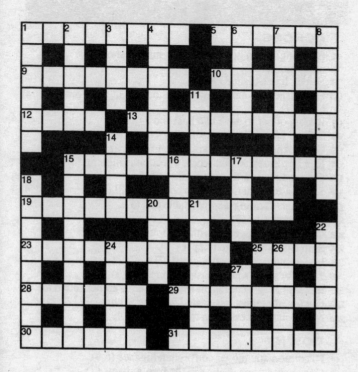

ACROSS

1 Hurrying with a good weapon to make a short observation (5,6)
9 Direct, like a bishop (7)
10 He finishes the number with one that might carry one away (7)
11 It's big of her to have two husbands! (3)
12 Stripped for a dingy retreat in action (7)
13 Gets to the point of feeling discomfort again (7)
14 Run into embankment where a section is missing (3)
15 Get ready to tear the end finally off (5)
17 Starting for America by ship could be hell! (5)
18 Bloomers forming a comfortable bed (5)
20 One alternative (5)
22 Only a fool can get by without money (3)
24 Ship Eve out in a bad temper (7)
25 Lower publicity in awful greed (7)
26 Time for some square-bashing in retreat (3)
27 Increase Meg's confusion when a relative comes round (7)
28 Got together those associated with the Right (7)
29 Not so much to eat when travelling cheaply (7,4)

DOWN

1 His diplomatic moves convey intelligence (6,9)
2 One shouldn't be dealing in the firm's shares (7)
3 Work to make some dough (5)
4 Labour leader with strange thin bray indicating where people can get lost (9)
5 Transport in driving rain can be bliss! (7)
6 It's heaven for those who aren't dead! (7,8)
7 Think quietly over the Berlin version (6)
8 Entertains applications before lunch (6)
16 Pitch rope out in view of what's coming (9)
18 Another chance to see a programme about fuel (6)
19 Holes up at last with an income (7)
21 Do badly coming up to change gear for robes (7)
23 Regular day set for moving (6)
25 Challenged to make an American prosecutor blush (5)

Solutions

1

ACROSS: 1 Home Counties, **8** Article, **9** Lunatic, **11** Elevations, **12** Tuna, **14** Ordained, **16** Recent, **17** Sum, **19** Subway, **21** Disorder, **24** Lois, **25** Diminuendo, **27** Evasion, **28** Animals, **29** Perfect tense.
DOWN: 1 Hothead, **2** Mechanical, **3** Crevices, **4** Upland, **5** Tony, **6** Extrude, **7** Mademoiselle, **10** Charterhouse, **13** Revolution, **15** Dud, **18** Militant, **20** Brigade, **22** Dentate, **23** Picnic, **26** Tiff.

2

ACROSS: 6 Ulterior motive, **9** Beamed, **10** Lodgings, **11** Cheapest, **13** Invite, **15** Office, **17** Oyster, **19** Ashlar, **20** Reversal, **22** Bursting, **24** Stride, **26** Merchant prince.
DOWN: 1 Jude the Obscure, **2** Item, **3** Bridle, **4** Smudgily, **5** Etui, **7** Oblate, **8** Vegetarian diet, **12** Awful, **14** Voter, **16** Carnival, **18** Fright, **21** Vestry, **23** Sack, **25** Rink.

3

ACROSS: 1 Derelict, **5** Shades, **9** Pole star, **10** Raisin, **12** Styx, **13** Directness, **15** Go as you please, **19** Harbour-master, **23** Prehensile, **25** Asti, **28** Exiles, **29** Pedigree, **30** Tights, **31** Stripper.
DOWN: 1 Depose, **2** Rally, **3** Lush, **4** Charity, **6** Heart, **7** Disrepair, **8** Sinister, **11** Beau, **14** Halo, **15** Gardening, **16** Ohm, **17** Lath, **18** Shipment, **20** Rush, **21** Ailment, **22** Linear, **24** Elect, **26** Scrap, **27** Fifi.

4

ACROSS: 1 Clear the air, **9** Limping, **10** Burglar, **11** Ice, **12** Squared, **13** Riveted, **14** Tot, **15** Media, **17** Liver, **18** Basic, **20** Shelf, **22** Pip, **24** Scrooge, **25** Cartoon, **26** Rah, **27** Rotunda, **28** Enamour, **29** Harvest moon.
DOWN: 1 Come up to scratch, **2** Epigram, **3** Rigid, **4** Hibernate, **5** Arrival, **6** Relative pronoun, **7** Closet, **8** Trader, **16** Desperate, **18** Bistro, **19** Crooner, **21** Farrago, **23** Penury, **25** Cheat.

5

ACROSS: 1 Student, **5** Pounce, **9** Address, **10** Leisure, **11** Par, **12** Sheet-anchor, **13** Ochre, **14** Ambergris, **16** Cowardice, **17** Video, **19** Dual control, **22** Aft, **23** Inherit, **24** Grandma, **26** Around, **27** Deluded.
DOWN: 1 Shampoo, **2** Under the weather, **3** Exe, **4** Taste, **5** Palatable, **6** Union, **7** Caught red-handed, **8** Hearts, **12** Sheer, **14** Alienated, **15** Revel, **16** Codlin, **18** Outward, **20** Corfu, **21** Raged, **25** Awl.

6

ACROSS: 1 Moral victory, **8** Pontiff, **9** Flutter, **11** Roustabout, **12** Sing, **14** Tutorial, **16** Knight, **17** Tom, **19** Moping, **21** Garrison, **24** Jury, **25** Periodical, **27** Built-in, **28** In brief, **29** Slow movement.
DOWN: 1 Manhunt, **2** Roistering, **3** Lifeboat, **4** Influx, **5** Taut, **6** Rotting, **7** Spare-time job, **10** Right and left, **13** Incredible, **15** Log, **18** Maritime, **20** Partial, **22** Sacrist, **23** Lean-to, **26** Stew.

7

ACROSS: 6 Listen to reason, **9** Streak, **10** Incubate, **11** Strident, **13** Bereft, **15** Evelyn, **17** Health, **19** Bertha, **20** Exercise, **22** Scrawled, **24** Employ, **26** Personal appeal.
DOWN: 1 Fly to the rescue, **2** Isle, **3** Heckle, **4** Crucible, **5** Lamb, **7** Thirty, **8** Out of this world, **12** Inept, **14** Relic, **16** Yearling, **18** Feudal, **21** Exempt, **23** Also, **25** Peek.

8

ACROSS: 1 Creative, **5** Gossip, **9** Portable, **10** Bounce, **12** Lily, **13** Fancy dress, **15** Save one's bacon, **19** Under Milk Wood, **23** Collection, **25** Stem, **28** August, **29** Parental, **30** Either, **31** Flattery.
DOWN: 1 Cupola, **2** Enrol, **3** Tram, **4** Volcano, **6** Ovoid, **7** Sentenced, **8** Pleasant, **11** Acre, **14** Aver, **15** Sidelight, **16** Nil, **17** Book, **18** Purchase, **20** Iota, **21** Know-all, **22** Smelly, **24** Ensue, **26** Title, **27** Meat.

9

ACROSS: 1 Go to Jericho, **9** Scourge, **10** Patient, **11** Roe, **12** Regress, **13** Leonine, **14** Yet, **15** Taste, **17** Eight, **18** Steam, **20** Batch, **22** Ebb, **24** Arousal, **25** Serpent, **26** Tip, **27** Burmese, **28** Oloroso, **29** Helen of Troy.
DOWN: 1 George the Fourth, **2** Torrent, **3** Jeers, **4** Repellent, **5** Cathode, **6** Opening ceremony, **7** Astray, **8** Attest, **16** Subaltern, **18** Shabby, **19** Misdeal, **21** Harbour, **23** Button, **25** Spoof.

10

ACROSS: 1 Climate, **5** Alarms, **9** Reached, **10** Chowder, **11** Cut, **12** Elephantine, **13** Sweat, **14** Coltishly, **16** Icelandic, **17** Romeo, **19** Scrumptious, **22** Tat, **23** Debauch, **24** Syringe, **26** Pet-top, **27** Tigress.
DOWN: 1 Caracas, **2** Ivan the Terrible, **3** Ash, **4** Endue, **5** Alcoholic, **6** Acorn, **7** Midnight matinee, **8** Creepy, **12** Extra, **14** Cadetship, **15** Idris, **16** Inside, **18** Outlets, **20** Mount, **21** Onset, **25** Rig.

11

ACROSS: 1 First attempt, **8** Alleged, **9** Rampant, **11** Fickleness, **12** Farm, **14** Flautist, **16** Shadow, **17** Sap, **19** Inflow, **21** Rainfall, **24** Tart, **25** Detachment, **27** Reserve, **28** Initial, **29** Red-letter day.
DOWN: 1 Felucca, **2** Regulation, **3** Tidiness, **4** Thrush, **5** Emma, **6** Placard, **7** Half of bitter, **10** Time will tell, **13** Shanghaied, **15** Tar, **18** Paradise, **20** Foresee, **22** Amenity, **23** Defect, **26** Oral.

12

ACROSS: 6 Hollow pretence, **9** Swerve, **10** Registry, **11** Off-break, **13** Nickel, **15** Trumps, **17** Aspect, **19** Census, **20** Abstract, **22** Ugliness, **24** Motion, **26** Three-bottle man.
DOWN: 1 Show of strength, **2** Blur, **3** Cohere, **4** Leggings, **5** Zeus, **7** Peruke, **8** Current account, **12** Bouts, **14** Cheer, **16** Passer-by, **18** Basset, **21** Simple, **23** Iced, **25** Time.

13

ACROSS: 1 Palisade, **5** Morsel, **9** Compress, **10** Inform, **12** Lute, **13** Cavalryman, **15** Record-breaker, **19** Ardent admirer, **23** Manipulate, **25** Line, **28** Shaman, **29** Politics, **30** Nation, **31** Skeleton.
DOWN: 1 Pickle, **2** Limit, **3** Sire, **4** Despair, **6** Owner, **7** Shoemaker, **8** Luminary, **11** Barb, **14** Icon, **15** Redundant, **16** Dad, **17** Earl, **18** Parmesan, **20** Ally, **21** Mattock, **22** Reason, **24** Piano, **26** Idiot, **27** Bill.

14

ACROSS: 1 Budding poet, **9** Trivial, **10** Natters, **11** Ace, **12** Dukedom, **13** Rampage, **14** Ova, **15** Edict, **17** Naked, **18** Cadet, **20** Paris, **22** Fir, **24** Profane, **25** Sitters, **26** Mop, **27** Outline, **28** Ashdown, **29** Right-angled.
DOWN: 1 Bricks and mortar, **2** Dwindle, **3** Islam, **4** Generator, **5** Ottoman, **6** The back of beyond, **7** Studio, **8** Ascend, **16** Implement, **18** Captor, **19** Tearing, **21** Satchel, **23** Resent, **25** Spain.

15

ACROSS: 1 Suspect, **5** Author, **9** Enforce, **10** Oldster, **11** Toe, **12** Categorical, **13** Cairn, **14** Initially, **16** Assonance, **17** Pilot, **19** Enlargement, **22** Urn, **23** Suntrap, **24** Hostile, **26** Dealer, **27** Cabinet.
DOWN: 1 Sceptic, **2** Suffer in silence, **3** Err, **4** Treat, **5** Alongside, **6** Tudor, **7** Optical illusion, **8** Frilly, **12** Canon, **14** Innkeeper, **15** Input, **16** Averse, **18** Tangent, **20** Rural, **21** Ethic, **25** Sob.

16

ACROSS: 1 Rolling stone, **8** Insight, **9** Disband, **11** Silk-screen, **12** Vase, **14** Margaret, **16** Harass, **17** Dom, **19** Lotion, **21** Munition, **24** Trap, **25** Discoursed, **27** Suffice, **28** Laid low, **29** Scriptwriter.

DOWN: 1 Rustler, **2** Legislator, **3** Interned, **4** Gadget, **5** Tosh, **6** Niagara, **7** Dissimulates, **10** Dressing-down, **13** Manicurist, **15** Tom, **18** Muscular, **20** Traffic, **22** Insular, **23** Divert, **26** Kiwi.

17

ACROSS: 6 New lease of life, **9** Dinner, **10** Tiresome, **11** One-piece, **13** Dismay, **15** Malady, **17** Ground, **19** Critic, **20** Traction, **22** Increase, **24** Curate, **26** Bristol fashion.

DOWN: 1 Ancient mariner, **2** Swan, **3** Decree, **4** Corridor, **5** Plus, **7** Setter, **8** Fame and fortune, **12** Pilot, **14** Stunt, **16** Dictator, **18** Itself, **21** Accuse, **23** Rasp, **25** Rain.

18

ACROSS: 1 Deadlock, **5** Splash, **9** Calabash, **10** Carbon, **12** Dawn, **13** Notionally, **15** Stiff sentence, **19** Engaging smile, **23** Transgress, **25** Adze, **28** Roused, **29** Deranged, **30** Sleepy, **31** Standard.

DOWN: 1 Decade, **2** Allow, **3** Lobe, **4** Cast-off, **6** Prawn, **7** Ambulance, **8** Honey-bee, **11** Fine, **14** King, **15** Signature, **16** Sag, **17** Trio, **18** Features, **20** Nark, **21** Suspect, **22** Mended, **24** Sheep, **26** Dogma, **27** Lawn.

19

ACROSS: 1 Wrong number, **9** Rosette, **10** Soupcon, **11** Elk, **12** Freeman, **13** Isotope, **14** Tin, **15** Local, **17** Right, **18** Tasks, **20** Under, **22** Bag, **24** Parting, **25** Deviate, **26** Ear, **27** Fraught, **28** Invited, **29** Horse-dealer.

DOWN: 1 Waste one's breath, **2** Optimal, **3** Green, **4** Unskilled, **5** Boudoir, **6** Rock of Gibraltar, **7** Profit, **8** Unrest, **16** Courgette, **18** Tip-off, **19** Swinger, **21** Revival, **23** Greedy, **25** Drive.

20

ACROSS: 1 Amusing, **5** Astute, **9** Oddment, **10** Hobnail, **11** Air, **12** Disarmament, **13** Orion, **14** Prevailed, **16** Recumbent, **17** Panel, **19** Desegregate, **22** Cam, **23** Swilled, **24** Lockout, **26** Onager, **27** Shocked.

DOWN: 1 Avocado, **2** Under discussion, **3** Ire, **4** Gates, **5** Abhorrent, **6** Tibia, **7** Travelling clock, **8** Slated, **12** Denim, **14** Pretender, **15** Apple, **16** Radish, **18** Limited, **20** Gulag, **21** Atlas, **25** Coo.

21

ACROSS: 1 Family circle, 8 Pirates, 9 Repress, 11 Shibboleth, 12 Mayo, 14 Legalise, 16 Hidden, 17 Sam, 19 Spouse, 21 Reaction, 24 Oath, 25 Proscenium, 27 Noodles, 28 Emirate, 29 Remonstrance.
DOWN: 1 Farming, 2 Metabolism, 3 Listless, 4 Curate, 5 Rope, 6 Leeward, 7 Apostle spoon, 10 Sworn enemies, 13 Discretion, 15 Ear, 18 Menswear, 20 Outcome, 22 Imitate, 23 Crisis, 26 Alto.

22

ACROSS: 6 Other fish to fry, 9 Fringe, 10 Mandarin, 11 Mistreat, 13 Larder, 15 Gerbil, 17 Dragon, 19 Potent, 20 Espresso, 22 Spectral, 24 Oracle, 26 See what happens.
DOWN: 1 Courting couple, 2 Thin, 3 Freeze, 4 Chandler, 5 Goya, 7 Inmate, 8 Raise one's glass, 12 Three, 14 Rogue, 16 Interval, 18 Health, 21 Prompt, 23 Cowl, 25 Apex.

23

ACROSS: 1 Blackout, 5 Jetsam, 9 Serenade, 10 Pounds, 12 Lull, 13 Deliberate, 15 Maids of honour, 19 Long time no see, 23 Grandstand, 25 Lamb, 28 Oregon, 29 Strangle, 30 Eleven, 31 Opponent.
DOWN: 1 Bustle, 2 April, 3 Kind, 4 Undress, 6 Erode, 7 Singapore, 8 Misheard, 11 Tiff, 14 Lift, 15 Manganese, 16 Owe, 17 Oust, 18 Flagpole, 20 Mite, 21 Nonstop, 22 Absent, 24 Drone, 26 Argue, 27 Sago.

24

ACROSS: 1 Peace of mind, 9 Tripper, 10 Abstain, 11 Log, 12 Anthony, 13 Egghead, 14 Doh, 15 Easel, 17 Tribe, 18 Meter, 20 Match, 22 Gab, 24 Dowager, 25 Clothes, 26 Ill, 27 Airport, 28 Ailment, 29 Dylan Thomas.
DOWN: 1 Paint the town red, 2 Approve, 3 Early, 4 Flageolet, 5 Insight, 6 Deafening cheers, 7 Strand, 8 On edge, 16 Samaritan, 18 Madras, 19 Rag-doll, 21 Hoodlum, 23 Basuto, 25 Clash.

25

ACROSS: 1 Cambric, 5 Callow, 9 Optimum, 10 Nuclear, 11 Hue, 12 Factory hand, 13 Thong, 14 Ferocious, 16 Prostrate, 17 Awake, 19 Nail-varnish, 22 Odd, 23 Edition, 24 Feather, 26 Inhere, 27 Retired.
DOWN: 1 Crochet, 2 Matter of opinion, 3 Rum, 4 Comic, 5 Concourse, 6 Lucky, 7 One way or another, 8 Brides, 12 Fight, 14 Fragrance, 15 Coach, 16 Ponder, 18 Endured, 20 Voice, 21 Infer, 25 Apt.

26

ACROSS: 1 Much mistaken, 8 Trainer, 9 Earmark, 11 Prime mover, 12 Cute, 14 Ingested, 16 Invent, 17 Dab, 19 Harrow, 21 Marriage, 24 Idle, 25 Fatalistic, 27 Granite, 28 Crazier, 29 State of siege.
DOWN: 1 Meaning, 2 Conversion, 3 Marooned, 4 Seeker, 5 Airy, 6 Erasure, 7 Stop fighting, 10 Keep the score, 13 Inordinate, 15 Dam, 18 Balances, 20 Reliant, 22 Astride, 23 Gazebo, 26 Sift.

27

ACROSS: 6 Take no interest, 9 Banana, 10 Fracture, 11 Streaker, 13 Nosing, 15 Chance, 17 Orient, 19 Cotton, 20 Location, 22 Floating, 24 Screws, 26 Bring to the boil.
DOWN: 1 Atlantic roller, 2 Skua, 3 Unpack, 4 Strainer, 5 Brat, 7 Infirm, 8 Strength of will, 12 Exact, 14 Spent, 16 Convicts, 18 Flight, 21 Cashew, 23 Anna, 25 Rood.

28

ACROSS: 1 Showdown, 5 Thwart, 9 Postmark, 10 Elapse, 12 Late, 13 Charioteer, 15 Stop-press news, 19 Other way round, 23 Understand, 25 Cave, 28 Enlist, 29 Discount, 30 Tudors, 31 Agitator.
DOWN: 1 Supply, 2 Onset, 3 Dump, 4 Worship, 6 Hello, 7 Apprehend, 8 Theorise, 11 True, 14 Door, 15 Scheduled, 16 Ray, 17 Soup, 18 Monument, 20 Anti, 21 Running, 22 Mentor, 24 Riser, 26 Adult, 27 Scut.

29

ACROSS: 1 Helping hand, 9 Squares, 10 October, 11 Emu, 12 Outcast, 13 Noisome, 14 Eon, 15 Aches, 17 Light, 18 Shrug, 20 Ruler, 22 Ask, 24 Deflate, 25 Attains, 26 Son, 27 Spanish, 28 Gravure, 29 Nerve-centre.
DOWN: 1 Haunting refrain, 2 Larnaca, 3 Inset, 4 Groundsel, 5 Ant-hill, 6 Debt of gratitude, 7 Ashore, 8 Arrest, 16 Horseshoe, 18 Sadist, 19 Glazier, 21 Retract, 23 Kismet, 25 Angle.

30

ACROSS: 1 Mobster, 5 Spring, 9 Dreamer, 10 Illicit, 11 Ink, 12 Inefficient, 13 Ashen, 14 Chequered, 16 Musicians, 17 Dread, 19 Self-defence, 22 Can, 23 Inn sign, 24 Vestige, 26 Wealth, 27 Lebanon.
DOWN: 1 Madeira, 2 Break the silence, 3 Tim, 4 Raree, 5 Stiffness, 6 Relic, 7 Nuclear reaction, 8 Stated, 12 Ionic, 14 Chaffinch, 15 Undue, 16 Mystic, 18 Dungeon, 20 Drill, 21 Novel, 25 Sob.

31

ACROSS: 1 Strip cartoon, **8** Apostle, **9** Reputed, **11** Authorship, **12** Hoot, **14** Creeping, **16** Fourth, **17** Tap, **19** Device, **21** Gazpacho, **24** Inch, **25** Mace-bearer, **27** Trotter, **28** Testing, **29** Ash Wednesday.
DOWN: 1 Scottle, **2** Retrospect, **3** Pleasant, **4** Afraid, **5** Type, **6** Outdoor, **7** Balanced diet, **10** Dutch courage, **13** Compressed, **15** Gag, **18** Patentee, **20** Vicious, **22** Certify, **23** Barred, **26** Stow.

32

ACROSS: 6 Leave of absence, **9** Annexe, **10** Overpaid, **11** Accolade, **13** Trunks, **15** Return, **17** Deduct, **19** Pro tem, **20** Cavalier, **22** Advocate, **24** Lock-up, **26** Desert one's post.
DOWN: 1 Blank cartridge, **2** Vale, **3** Geneva, **4** Absentee, **5** Keep, **7** Flower, **8** Cricket results, **12** Octet, **14** Usual, **16** Ramparts, **18** Screen, **21** Valise, **23** Open, **25** Cool.

33

ACROSS: 1 Regicide, **5** Player, **9** Porpoise, **10** Hatred, **12** Step, **13** Fantasises, **15** Strong backing, **19** Local landmark, **23** Practising, **25** Emir, **28** Ruined, **29** Midnight, **30** Patter, **31** Stoppage.
DOWN: 1 Repose, **2** Gorse, **3** Crow, **4** Disdain, **6** Leads, **7** Yardstick, **8** Redesign, **11** Stub, **14** Oral, **15** Socialist, **16** Gun, **17** Char, **18** Claptrap, **20** Also, **21** Dentist, **22** Writhe, **24** There, **26** Magma, **27** Snap.

34

ACROSS: 1 Filthy lucre, **9** Parable, **10** Swindle, **11** Lot, **12** Relates, **13** Doleful, **14** Ego, **15** Refit, **17** Dandy, **18** Alert, **20** Other, **24** Sir, **24** Cowslip, **25** Oddment, **26** Ram, **27** Portico, **28** Epithet, **29** High feather.
DOWN: 1 For all one's worth, **2** Lobster, **3** Heels, **4** Last ditch, **5** Chilled, **6** End of one's tether, **7** Sparse, **8** Replay, **16** Foolproof, **18** Accept, **19** Telling, **21** Reddish, **23** Rotate, **25** Omega.

35

ACROSS: 1 Decibel, **5** Recite, **9** Grounds, **10** Taverna, **11** Aid, **12** Distinction, **13** Sauce, **14** Tremulous, **16** Nakedness, **17** Inert, **19** Proportions, **22** Gig, **23** Imagine, **24** Satiate, **26** Advert, **27** Success.
DOWN: 1 Dog tags, **2** Cloud-cuckoo-land, **3** Bun, **4** Loses, **5** Retainers, **6** Civic, **7** Turn in one's grave, **8** Paints, **12** Dread, **14** Treatment, **15** Units, **16** Napkin, **18** Tigress, **20** Olive, **21** Oasis, **25** Tic.

36

ACROSS: 1 Going concern, 8 Maestro, 9 Enlists, 11 Needlessly, 12 Mini, 14 Fastener, 16 Spinet, 17 Sap, 19 Inmate, 21 Temporal, 24 Nark, 25 Innumerate, 27 Secular, 28 Intwine, 29 Monkey-tricks.

DOWN: 1 Geezers, 2 Intellects, 3 Glossies, 4 Openly, 5 Call, 6 Russian, 7 Among friends, 10 Shirt-sleeves, 13 Apoplectic, 15 Rat, 18 Peculiar, 20 Morocco, 22 Roadies, 23 Energy, 26 Flak.

37

ACROSS: 6 Husband and wife, 9 Attend, 10 Triangle, 11 Heighten, 13 Anchor, 15 Trench, 17 Medium, 19 Piston, 20 Reliable, 22 Balmoral, 24 Repeat, 26 Perfect example.

DOWN: 1 That certain age, 2 Isle, 3 Bandit, 4 Intimate, 5 Swan, 7 Doting, 8 Follow-my-leader, 12 Guest, 14 China, 16 Contract, 18 Grilse, 21 Lariat, 23 Muff, 25 Pipe.

38

ACROSS: 1 Hiawatha, 5 Swipes, 9 Car ferry, 10 Stroke, 12 Tank, 13 Sweetheart, 15 Advance notice, 19 Home Secretary, 23 Ridiculous, 25 Eton, 28 Unlock, 29 Adorable, 30 Hookah, 31 Freetown.

DOWN: 1 Hecate, 2 Apron, 3 Anew, 4 Hard-won, 6 Watch, 7 Profanity, 8 Sheathed, 11 Cede, 14 Avis, 15 Armadillo, 16 Cur, 17 Opal, 18 Thorough, 20 Call, 21 Ecuador, 22 Unseen, 24 Cocoa, 26 Taboo, 27 True.

39

ACROSS: 1 Cakes and ale, 9 Rampage, 10 Subject, 11 Nut, 12 Outside, 13 Immoral, 14 Yet, 15 Haste, 17 Newts, 18 Dress, 20 Aisle, 22 War, 24 Tremble, 25 Serpent, 26 Set, 27 Uncouth, 28 Eminent, 29 Escaping gas.

DOWN: 1 Come to the rescue, 2 Knavish, 3 Scene, 4 Nastiness, 5 Albumen, 6 Eyebrow tweezers, 7 Priory, 8 Stalls, 16 Spaceship, 18 Detour, 19 Subfusc, 21 Earring, 23 Rotate, 25 Stern.

40

ACROSS: 1 Pointed, 5 Cerise, 9 Indiana, 10 Allegro, 11 Boa, 12 Dilapidated, 13 Egret, 14 Profusely, 16 Asparagus, 17 Cliff, 19 Alternative, 22 Gig, 23 Elitist, 24 Glamour, 26 Skinny, 27 Tapered.

DOWN: 1 Pliable, 2 Indian rope-trick, 3 Tea, 4 Drawl, 5 Champions, 6 Ruled, 7 Sightseeing tour, 8 Monday, 12 Deter, 14 Pageantry, 15 Uncle, 16 Abated, 18 Figured, 20 Reign, 21 Ingot, 25 Asp.

41

ACROSS: 1 Dictatorship, **8** Feelers, **9** Pull off, **11** Triangular, **12** Fist, **14** Engrafts, **16** Auntie, **17** Sow, **19** Escudo, **21** Barbaric, **24** Oath, **25** Forecaster, **27** Declaim, **28** Lattice, **29** Second course.
DOWN: 1 Dieting, **2** Clean hands, **3** Assaults, **4** Orphan, **5** Sold, **6** Ironist, **7** Off the record, **10** Fitted carpet, **13** Dumb-waiter, **15** Sob, **18** Waterloo, **20** Cuticle, **22** Ratline, **23** Doomed, **26** Faro.

42

ACROSS: 6 Negative equity, **9** Weight, **10** Thespian, **11** Assessor, **13** Timing, **15** Assign, **17** Crocus, **19** Meteor, **20** Firearms, **22** Semolina, **24** Nectar, **26** Starboard watch.
DOWN: 1 Understatement, **2** Agog, **3** Status, **4** Selector, **5** Lump, **7** Votary, **8** Tea and sympathy, **12** Ensue, **14** Mocha, **16** Garrison, **18** Affair, **21** Renown, **23** Ours, **25** City.

43

ACROSS: 1 Diatribe, **5** Bandit, **9** Fortress, **10** Sequel, **12** Cowl, **13** Forefather, **15** Friend at court, **19** On bended knees, **23** Flightless, **25** Tsar, **28** Italic, **29** Armoured, **30** Treaty, **31** Flagrant.
DOWN: 1 Deface, **2** Arrow, **3** Rare, **4** Bassoon, **6** Arena, **7** Doughnuts, **8** Tolerate, **11** Hera, **14** Lion, **15** Fabricate, **16** Dud, **17** Chew, **18** Conflict, **20** Ella, **21** Kestrel, **22** Credit, **24** Hoist, **26** Syria, **27** Long.

44

ACROSS: 1 Bolt upright, **9** Redound, **10** Thrower, **11** Ego, **12** Manager, **13** Unearth, **14** Rub, **15** Rajah, **17** Tenor, **18** Shelf, **20** Video, **22** Pub, **24** Unknown, **25** Defused, **26** Ice, **27** Glacial, **28** Necking, **29** Tetrahedron.
DOWN: 1 Bed and breakfast, **2** Lounger, **3** Under, **4** Retouched, **5** Garment, **6** Towering passion, **7** Cromer, **8** Archer, **16** Juvenilia, **18** Smudge, **19** Florist, **21** Officer, **23** Bodega, **25** Dense.

45

ACROSS: 1 Decides, **5** Damson, **9** Seminar, **10** Segment, **11** Ado, **12** Reproachful, **13** Token, **14** Greenhorn, **16** Dromedary, **17** Gamma, **19** Enlargement, **22** Eel, **23** Mediate, **24** Seaside, **26** Senses, **27** Delight.
DOWN: 1 Descant, **2** Common knowledge, **3** Don, **4** Scrap, **5** Discovery, **6** Magic, **7** Overflow meeting, **8** Stolen, **12** Range, **14** Graceless, **15** Night, **16** Dreamy, **18** Ailment, **20** Roams, **21** Eased, **25** Awl.

46

ACROSS: 1 Vainglorious, 8 Miniver, 9 Trussed, 11 Relegation, 12 Fuss, 14 Charring, 16 Tender, 17 Gum, 19 Twenty, 21 Navigate, 24 Orgy, 25 Counteract, 27 Station, 28 Traject, 29 Idiosyncrasy.

DOWN: 1 Vanilla, 2 Invigorate, 3 Gyrating, 4 Option, 5 Irun, 6 Unsound, 7 Imprecations, 10 Disorientate, 13 Desiderata, 15 Gun, 18 Magnetic, 20 England, 22 Academy, 23 Bounty, 26 Lido.

47

ACROSS: 6 Leading actress, 9 Panama, 10 Beautify, 11 Stockade, 13 Bereft, 15 Excuse, 17 Lesser, 19 Arrest, 20 Artistic, 22 Sundered, 24 Alight, 26 Address unknown.

DOWN: 1 Clear the ground, 2 Papa, 3 Cicada, 4 Scramble, 5 Fret, 7 Goblet, 8 Soft furnishing, 12 Cache, 14 Risks, 16 Satirist, 18 Landau, 21 Thanks, 23 Dirt, 25 Icon.

48

ACROSS: 1 Face-lift, 5 Probed, 9 Compound, 10 Amazon, 12 Oily, 13 Intestinal, 15 Ask permission, 19 Right up to date, 23 Mastermind, 25 Scar, 28 Spiral, 29 Absolute, 30 Deepen, 31 Assemble.

DOWN: 1 Factor, 2 Camel, 3 Look, 4 Finance, 6 Remit, 7 Byzantine, 8 Dangling, 11 Term, 14 Skit, 15 Augustine, 16 Rot, 17 Snag, 18 Promised, 20 Pump, 21 Omnibus, 22 Freeze, 24 Elate, 26 Crumb, 27 Love.

49

ACROSS: 1 Bed and board, 9 Glimmer, 10 Outgrow, 11 Sit, 12 Enhance, 13 Haircut, 14 Dip, 15 Cheer, 17 Edith, 18 Sport, 20 Crypt, 22 Nod, 24 Imperil, 25 Tearing, 26 Lei, 27 Cockade, 28 Besides, 29 Scout-master.

DOWN: 1 Bright prospects, 2 Demonic, 3 Nurse, 4 Brotherly, 5 Astride, 6 Direction finder, 7 Agreed, 8 Twitch, 16 Excellent, 18 Stitch, 19 Tornado, 21 Transit, 23 Digest, 25 Tibia.

50

ACROSS: 1 Shopper, 5 Basque, 9 Abandon, 10 Fearful, 11 Log, 12 Alexandrine, 13 Woman, 14 Croissant, 16 Paralysis, 17 Raven, 19 Elaboration, 22 Nag, 23 Seaside, 24 Carnage, 26 Recess, 27 Retreat.

DOWN: 1 Swallow, 2 Orange marmalade, 3 Pad, 4 Rinse, 5 Buffaloes, 6 Stand, 7 Unfair advantage, 8 Client, 12 Annul, 14 Castanets, 15 Siren, 16 Please, 18 Neglect, 20 Ovine, 21 Incur, 25 Rut.

51

ACROSS: **1** Rich relation, **8** Attract, **9** Minutes, **11** Telepathic, **12** Dram, **14** Shrugged, **16** Hoop-la, **17** Dab, **19** Carboy, **21** Yarmouth, **24** Orgy, **25** Topiarists, **27** Symbols, **28** Omicron, **29** Unwritten law.
DOWN: **1** Rattler, **2** Champignon, **3** Retitled, **4** Limpid, **5** Tang, **6** Outcrop, **7** Maltese cross, **10** Sympathising, **13** Commercial, **15** Day, **18** Baritone, **20** Regimen, **22** Unscrew, **23** Corset, **26** Four.

52

ACROSS: **6** Lick one's wounds, **9** Pistol, **10** Disgorge, **11** Daughter, **13** Inland, **15** Drench, **17** Parish, **19** Bistro, **20** Anathema, **22** Apparent, **24** Talent, **26** Medicine bottle.
DOWN: **1** Plain and simple, **2** Scot, **3** Goblet, **4** Swastika, **5** Ludo, **7** Endure, **8** Dog in the manger, **12** Guest, **14** Leith, **16** Choleric, **18** Castle, **21** Action, **23** Avid, **25** Late.

53

ACROSS: **1** Half-time, **5** Nutmeg, **9** Contrary, **10** Fiance, **12** Even, **13** Inconstant, **15** Reincarnation, **19** Surprise party, **23** Idealistic, **25** Stay, **28** Athens, **29** Carapace, **30** Towing, **31** Pendulum.
DOWN: **1** Hockey, **2** Lunge, **3** Turf, **4** Moronic, **6** Units, **7** Mendacity, **8** Greeting, **11** Poor, **14** Bier, **15** Raree-show, **16** Ape, **17** Acre, **18** Aspirant, **20** Sash, **21** Primate, **22** Lyceum, **24** Linen, **26** Trail, **27** Wand.

54

ACROSS: **1** Pass the buck, **9** Own goal, **10** Entwine, **11** Ear, **12** Neither, **13** Gunshot, **14** Bus, **15** Ripen, **17** Drone, **18** Sharp, **20** Kneel, **22** Tub, **24** Impious, **25** Secrete, **26** Tot, **27** Mandela, **28** Average, **29** Rabbit-punch.
DOWN: **1** Pencil-sharpener, **2** Smother, **3** Tiler, **4** Emergence, **5** Untuned, **6** Knight of the bath, **7** Hobnob, **8** Mettle, **16** Pakistani, **18** Shimmy, **19** Proverb, **21** Lectern, **23** Brewer, **25** Stamp.

55

ACROSS: **1** Private, **5** Incise, **9** Re-elect, **10** Tearful, **11** Tar, **12** Exaggerated, **13** Shawl, **14** Gratified, **16** Appendage, **17** Agnes, **19** Perpetually, **22** Man, **23** Egotist, **24** Relieve, **26** Gratis, **27** Creases.
DOWN: **1** Pirates, **2** Ice-cream parlour, **3** Age, **4** Extra, **5** Integrate, **6** Chair, **7** Safety in numbers, **8** Glided, **12** Ellen, **14** Graduates, **15** Italy, **16** Apples, **18** Singers, **20** Exist, **21** Lyric, **25** Lie.

56

ACROSS: 1 Mount Everest, **8** Risible, **9** Nourish, **11** Emancipate, **12** Sing, **14** Psalmist, **16** Hang-up, **17** Sat, **19** Outing, **21** Pastiche, **24** Iron, **25** Centurions, **27** Extract, **28** Counter, **29** Bridge player.
DOWN: 1 Mascara, **2** Unbecoming, **3** Trespass, **4** Vanity, **5** Rout, **6** Sailing, **7** Greek profile, **10** High-pressure, **13** Canterbury, **15** Tap, **18** Tactical, **20** Trotter, **22** Crofter, **23** Settle, **26** Hand.

57

ACROSS: 6 Initial attempt, **9** Untrue, **10** Viennese, **11** Sculptor, **13** Affray, **15** Expect, **17** Behind, **19** Effete, **20** Et cetera, **22** Daughter, **24** Ambush, **26** Self-possession.
DOWN: 1 Pinnacle of fame, **2** Tier, **3** Digest, **4** Steerage, **5** Dean, **7** Livery, **8** Past and present, **12** Lapse, **14** Feint, **16** Creation, **18** Debris, **21** Clause, **23** Gift, **25** Bait.

58

ACROSS: 1 Sob-stuff, **5** Muriel, **9** Stallion, **10** Shrimp, **12** Eddy, **13** Dispatched, **15** Mild and bitter, **19** Hard to swallow, **23** Squandered, **25** Dais, **28** Idiots, **29** Moderate, **30** Enlist, **31** Vestment.
DOWN: 1 System, **2** Braid, **3** Till, **4** Florida, **6** Unhit, **7** Irish stew, **8** Lapidary, **11** Aped, **14** Plot, **15** Mercurial, **16** Now, **17** Idly, **18** Chastise, **20** Shed, **21** Awesome, **22** Ascent, **24** Notes, **26** Agate, **27** Beat.

59

ACROSS: 1 Play the game, **9** Turn-out, **10** Portent, **11** Ore, **12** Brother, **13** Doubter, **14** Elm, **15** Ruche, **17** Daisy, **18** Dined, **20** Catch, **22** Bus, **24** Buffalo, **25** Bravado, **26** Tea, **27** Sweater, **28** Cricket, **29** Second-sight.
DOWN: 1 Performing fleas, **2** Another, **3** Tutor, **4** Expedient, **5** Aground, **6** Electric blanket, **7** Stable, **8** Sturdy, **16** Cyclotron, **18** Debase, **19** Drastic, **21** Hearing, **23** Smooth, **25** Backs.

60

ACROSS: 1 Apropos, **5** Patent, **9** Prudent, **10** Inertia, **11** Rod, **12** Contentious, **13** Defer, **14** Freeboard, **16** Repossess, **17** Yacht, **19** Billsticker, **22** Ski, **23** Rousing, **24** Torture, **26** Gentry, **27** Hayseed.
DOWN: 1 Aspired, **2** Round of applause, **3** Pie, **4** Satan, **5** Priceless, **6** Trent, **7** National costume, **8** Passed, **12** Cards, **14** Feelingly, **15** Buyer, **16** Robert, **18** Tail-end, **20** Stint, **21** Ketch, **25** Ray.

61

ACROSS: 1 Snake-charmer, **8** Relates, **9** Present, **11** Viewfinder, **12** Lama, **14** Manacles, **16** Pundit, **17** Sic, **19** Signal, **21** Rampages, **24** Arab, **25** Councillor, **27** Exploit, **28** Brigand, **29** Leading light.
DOWN: 1 Silvern, **2** Artificial, **3** Essences, **4** Hopper, **5** Rhea, **6** Emerald, **7** Grave mistake, **10** Tear to shreds, **13** Surprising, **15** Sir, **18** Cannibal, **20** Grapple, **22** Gallant, **23** Bolton, **26** Good.

62

ACROSS: 6 Robinson Crusoe, **9** Advent, **10** Fatality, **11** Defender, **13** Rebuff, **15** Nature, **17** Remain, **19** Stores, **20** Restless, **22** Chaplain, **24** Copper, **26** Critical moment.
DOWN: 1 Cradle-snatcher, **2** Able, **3** United, **4** Scot-free, **5** Pull, **7** Oxford, **8** Out of one's depth, **12** Enter, **14** Brawl, **16** Research, **18** Brunel, **21** Sector, **23** Path, **25** Pier.

63

ACROSS: 1 Seascape, **5** Savant, **9** Provided, **10** Compel, **12** Lute, **13** Prospector, **15** Country cousin, **19** Near neighbour, **23** Peashooter, **25** Olga, **28** Rattle, **29** Cogitate, **30** Duress, **31** Unsteady.
DOWN: 1 Supply, **2** About, **3** Chip, **4** Pierrot, **6** Alone, **7** Appetiser, **8** Tolerant, **11** Espy, **14** Burn, **15** Character, **16** Rag, **17** Oboe, **18** Inspired, **20** Iron, **21** Hoedown, **22** Napery, **24** Holes, **26** Liana, **27** Lift.

64

ACROSS: 1 Grain of sand, **9** Combine, **10** Overfed, **11** Dog, **12** Ecstasy, **13** Meeting, **14** Set, **15** Lower, **17** Souls, **18** Hinge, **20** Other, **22** Tap, **24** Rummage, **25** Catcher, **26** Nay, **27** On trial, **28** Confine, **29** Hand-grenade.
DOWN: 1 Game set and match, **2** Abigail, **3** Needy, **4** Frog-march, **5** Ageless, **6** Difficult choice, **7** Access, **8** Adages, **16** Wooden leg, **18** Harrow, **19** Elation, **21** Rotunda, **23** Porter, **25** Cycle.

65

ACROSS: 1 Incubus, **5** Drifts, **9** Naughty, **10** Mongrel, **11** Rut, **12** Inefficient, **13** Dross, **14** Plus-fours, **16** Conferred, **17** Baker, **19** Interrogate, **22** Tom, **23** Cripple, **24** Outsell, **26** Agency, **27** Theists.
DOWN: 1 Ignored, **2** Count for nothing, **3** Bah, **4** Style, **5** Dumbfound, **6** Ionic, **7** Three Musketeers, **8** Plates, **12** Issue, **14** Purposely, **15** Fable, **16** Clinch, **18** Rambles, **20** Ripen, **21** Aloft, **25** Toe.

66

ACROSS: 1 Reserved seat, 8 Opposes, 9 Garland, 11 Brigandage, 12 Omen, 14 Training, 16 Behalf, 17 Tub, 19 Regent, 21 Mismatch, 24 Oars, 25 Frolicsome, 27 Shannon, 28 Welcome, 29 Demi-mondaine.

DOWN: 1 Replica, 2 Sustaining, 3 Resident, 4 Engage, 5 Sort, 6 Anaemia, 7 Combat troops, 10 Den of thieves, 13 Vermicelli, 15 Gum, 18 Billowed, 20 Germane, 22 Two-tone, 23 Pronto, 26 Anti.

67

ACROSS: 6 Worthy of remark, 9 Propel, 10 Adoption, 11 Assuming, 13 Rummer, 15 Accost, 17 Adonis, 19 Sleepy, 20 Upheaval, 22 Swanking, 24 Remedy, 26 Precious little.

DOWN: 1 Sword-swallower, 2 Drop, 3 Chilli, 4 Armoured, 5 Emit, 7 Orange, 8 Rhode Island Red, 12 Uncle, 14 Mania, 16 Sky-pilot, 18 Fungus, 21 Horrid, 23 Neck, 25 Mate.

68

ACROSS: 1 Black eye, 5 Scotch, 9 Syracuse, 10 Cosmic, 12 Link, 13 Immortelle, 15 Stick-in-the-mud, 19 Even things out, 23 Unkindness, 25 Argo, 28 Really, 29 Outright, 30 Drying, 31 Defender.

DOWN: 1 Bustle, 2 Apron, 3 Kick, 4 Yashmak, 6 Clout, 7 Time limit, 8 Hacienda, 11 Boon, 14 List, 15 Speak-easy, 16 Inn, 17 Hook, 18 Required, 20 Iona, 21 Gesture, 22 Doctor, 24 Nylon, 26 Rigid, 27 Erie.

69

ACROSS: 1 Wedding-ring, 9 Panache, 10 Envelop, 11 Pay, 12 Inspect, 13 Berserk, 14 Tor, 15 Sepia, 17 Ethos, 18 Adele, 20 Rider, 22 Nip, 24 Towpath, 25 Riposte, 26 Era, 27 Tipster, 28 Diorama, 29 Reconnoitre.

DOWN: 1 Windscreen wiper, 2 Duchess, 3 Inept, 4 Greybeard, 5 Inverse, 6 Golden handshake, 7 Sprint, 8 Spokes, 16 Percheron, 18 Astute, 19 Elastic, 21 Rapport, 23 Pre-war, 25 Radio.

70

ACROSS: 1 Fall out, 5 Direct, 9 Scandal, 10 Scalene, 11 Use, 12 Non-partisan, 13 Enter, 14 Soapstone, 16 Prosecute, 17 Acrid, 19 Inheritance, 22 All, 23 Confide, 24 Mastery, 26 Recess, 27 Denoted.

DOWN: 1 Fissure, 2 Leave it to chance, 3 Odd, 4 Talon, 5 Disparate, 6 Roast, 7 Chess tournament, 8 Seance, 12 Nerve, 14 Squatters, 15 Stage, 16 Prince, 18 Delayed, 20 Rhine, 21 Nomad, 25 Sin.

71

ACROSS: **1** False economy, **8** Upright, **9** Visitor, **11** Inveterate, **12** Less, **14** Acrimony, **16** Presto, **17** Gem, **19** Sedate, **21** War-horse, **24** Oust, **25** Progenitor, **27** Evading, **28** Animate, **29** Announcement.

DOWN: **1** Forever, **2** Legitimate, **3** Entering, **4** Cavity, **5** Nest, **6** Matters, **7** Musical score, **10** Restore order, **13** Prehensile, **15** Yew, **18** Margrave, **20** Disdain, **22** Retract, **23** Origin, **26** Silo.

72

ACROSS: **6** Raised eyebrows, **9** Unkind, **10** Salesman, **11** Disburse, **13** Nought, **15** Guards, **17** Proper, **19** Crisis, **20** Contrary, **22** Purchase, **24** Droopy, **26** Chief constable.

DOWN: **1** Drinking trough, **2** Mimi, **3** Leader, **4** Berliner, **5** Iris, **7** Easter, **8** Weather prophet, **12** Brass, **14** Upper, **16** Distance, **18** Screen, **21** Nudity, **23** Crew, **25** Orbs.

73

ACROSS: **1** Foremost, **5** Carpet, **9** Military, **10** Opener, **12** Urdu, **13** Upper-class, **15** Words of wisdom, **19** Hard to believe, **23** Exhibition, **25** Ache, **28** Ideals, **29** Paradise, **30** Hasten, **31** Addendum.

DOWN: **1** Famous, **2** Ruled, **3** Mite, **4** Stripes, **6** Aspic, **7** Panhandle, **8** Tiresome, **11** Serf, **14** Writ, **15** Worthless, **16** Ode, **17** Iced, **18** Sheepish, **20** Bite, **21** Leopard, **22** Redeem, **24** Bulge, **26** Child, **27** Cake.

74

ACROSS: **1** Dead certain, **9** Outworn, **10** Flutter, **11** All, **12** Bristol, **13** Episode, **14** Egg, **15** Enact, **17** Erase, **18** Swing, **20** Rural, **22** Gap, **24** Sustain, **25** Lorelei, **26** Ada, **27** Abysmal, **28** Spiders, **29** Erroneously.

DOWN: **1** Do things in style, **2** Apostle, **3** Canal, **4** Reflector, **5** Abusive, **6** National Gallery, **7** Cobble, **8** Frieze, **16** Adrenalin, **18** Sashay, **19** Grammar, **21** Lorries, **23** Priest, **25** Lasso.

75

ACROSS: **1** Demerit, **5** Renown, **9** Perfect, **10** Puritan, **11** Sue, **12** Belly-dancer, **13** Tonic, **14** Open-armed, **16** Good night, **17** Oiled, **19** Mind-bending, **22** Mop, **23** Intones, **24** Advance, **26** Censor, **27** Osmosis.

DOWN: **1** Deposit, **2** Marie Antoinette, **3** Rye, **4** Total, **5** Repayment, **6** Norma, **7** With compliments, **8** Inured, **12** Bacon, **14** Organiser, **15** Along, **16** Gambit, **18** Depress, **20** Bonus, **21** Idaho, **25** Vim.

76

ACROSS: 1 Working party, 8 Ignited, 9 Orchard, 11 Propellant, 12 Stun, 14 Erecting, 16 Course, 17 Tub, 19 Novena, 21 Millrace, 24 Wire, 25 Headstrong, 27 Routine, 28 Version, 29 Elgin marbles.
DOWN: 1 Winsome, 2 Retreating, 3 Indolent, 4 Ground, 5 Arch, 6 Traitor, 7 Simple answer, 10 Donkey-engine, 13 Collateral, 15 Gum, 18 Bind over, 20 Virtual, 22 Agonies, 23 Redeem, 26 Kiwi.

77

ACROSS: 6 Food for thought, 9 Winkle, 10 Vermouth, 11 Listless, 13 Unsung, 15 Legume, 17 Cherub, 19 Hearts, 20 Ultimate, 22 Trombone, 24 Rocket, 26 Studio audience.
DOWN: 1 Official secret, 2 Fork, 3 Effete, 4 Thorough, 5 Judo, 7 Revise, 8 Hot and bothered, 12 Tiger, 14 Strum, 16 Mastodon, 18 Bureau, 21 Torrid, 23 Mode, 25 Cane.

78

ACROSS: 1 Quayside, 5 Mother, 9 Antelope, 10 Tarmac, 12 Nick, 13 Forecaster, 15 State of nature, 19 Peace offering, 23 Cheapskate, 25 Blot, 28 Log-jam, 29 Stripper, 30 Darken, 31 Feathers.
DOWN: 1 Quaint, 2 Attic, 3 Salt, 4 Deplore, 6 Omaha, 7 Hamstrung, 8 Recorder, 11 Leaf, 14 Wake, 15 Scavenger, 16 Oaf, 17 Acid, 18 Speckled, 20 Fake, 21 Entitle, 22 Storks, 24 Place, 26 Lapse, 27 Diet.

79

ACROSS: 1 Double Dutch, 9 Hardens, 10 Service, 11 Top, 12 Waiters, 13 Epithet, 14 Rio, 15 Sacks, 17 Globe, 18 Layer, 20 Indus, 22 Fad, 24 Caution, 25 Flotsam, 26 Too, 27 Scuttle, 28 Raining, 29 Barrel-organ.
DOWN: 1 Dormitory suburb, 2 Useless, 3 Lists, 4 Dispersed, 5 Turning, 6 Height of fashion, 7 Shower, 8 Settle, 16 Clientele, 18 Locust, 19 Roister, 21 Scoring, 23 Damage, 25 Forgo.

80

ACROSS: 1 Glisten, 5 Talent, 9 Romance, 10 Augment, 11 Air, 12 Spectacular, 13 Scion, 14 Subjugate, 16 Tangerine, 17 Dodge, 19 Predecessor, 22 Hod, 23 Lettuce, 24 Amateur, 26 Brutus, 27 Grandee.
DOWN: 1 Germans, 2 Immersion heater, 3 Ton, 4 Niece, 5 Tractable, 6 Logic, 7 Needle and thread, 8 Starve, 12 Singe, 14 Spineless, 15 Under, 16 Tipple, 18 Endorse, 20 Erupt, 21 Slang, 25 Ada.

81

ACROSS: 1 Tape-recorder, 8 Airport, 9 Amalgam, 11 Brute force, 12 Anon, 14 Grenades, 16 Massif, 17 Dub, 19 Palace, 21 Meringue, 24 Toga, 25 Assignment, 27 Hot line, 28 Vintner, 29 Cylinder-head.

DOWN: 1 Torture, 2 Provenance, 3 Rationed, 4 Chance, 5 Road, 6 Engines, 7 Cabbage patch, 10 Man of letters, 13 Malignance, 15 Sum, 18 Believer, 20 Lightly, 22 Gleaned, 23 Ascend, 26 Fifi.

82

ACROSS: 6 Highway robbery, 9 Intend, 10 Negative, 11 Defiance, 13 Vienna, 15 Salute, 17 Sneeze, 19 Firmer, 20 Identify, 22 Smacking, 24 Candid, 26 Traveller's tale.

DOWN: 1 Channel swimmer, 2 Ague, 3 Sweden, 4 Forgiven, 5 Abet, 7 Yankee, 8 Revenue officer, 12 Islam, 14 Erect, 16 Terrible, 18 Single, 21 Excuse, 23 Cove, 25 Noah.

83

ACROSS: 1 Handsome, 5 Sadist, 9 Particle, 10 Tunnel, 12 Even, 13 Adventurer, 15 High churchman, 19 Opposite sides, 23 Pickpocket, 25 Spur, 28 Entail, 29 Pinafore, 30 Scheme, 31 Offshoot.

DOWN: 1 Happen, 2 Nerve, 3 Slip, 4 Melodic, 6 Adult, 7 Ignoramus, 8 Tolerant, 11 Beau, 14 Ages, 15 Hopscotch, 16 Hue, 17 Code, 18 Compress, 20 Tuck, 21 Sheriff, 22 Arrest, 24 Prism, 26 Photo, 27 Bass.

84

ACROSS: 1 Quick glance, 9 Oversee, 10 Bertram, 11 Amy, 12 Denuded, 13 Reaches, 14 Ram, 15 Ripen, 17 Abyss, 18 Roses, 20 Other, 22 Ass, 24 Peevish, 25 Degrade, 26 Era, 27 Augment, 28 Rallied, 29 Reduced fare.

DOWN: 1 Queen's messenger, 2 Insider, 3 Knead, 4 Labyrinth, 5 Nirvana, 6 Earthly paradise, 7 Ponder, 8 Amuses, 16 Prophetic, 18 Repeat, 19 Stipend, 21 Regalia, 23 Steady, 25, Dared.